Problem Solving
Book B

MATH TO KNOW

GREAT SOURCE
EDUCATION GROUP
A Houghton Mifflin Company
New Ways to Know®

Developing

thinking skills through

READING and **WRITING**

Acknowledgments and Credits

Acknowledgments

Reviewers:

Cathy Bernhard
  District Program Facilitator–Title I Math
  Beaverton School District
  Beaverton, OR

Kathi Hudson
  Fourth Grade Teacher
  North Wayne Elementary School
  Metropolitan School District of Wayne
  Township
  Indianapolis, IN

Louise Muscarella-Daxon
  District Mathematics Supervisor
  Miami-Dade County Public Schools
  Miami, FL

Judy Peede
  Elementary Lead Math Teacher
  Wake County Public Schools
  Raleigh, NC

Beth Spivey
  Elementary Lead Math Teacher
  Wake County Public Schools
  Raleigh, NC

Lon M. Stettler
  Assistant Superintendent for Curriculum,
  Instruction, and Assessment
  Princeton City School District
  Cincinnati, OH

Credits

Writing: Justine Dunn, Judy Vandegrift

Review: Edward Manfre

Editorial: Carol DeBold, Pearl Ling, Susan Rogalski

Design/Production: Taurins Design

Creative Art: Alex Farquharson *pages 2, 3, 4, 23, 26, 37, 58, 65, 67, 74.* Greg Harris *pages 11, 19, 20, 72, 76, 81, 87.* Amanda Harvey *pages 14, 22, 32, 39, 54, 56, 71, 82.* Eileen Hine *icons.* Steve Mach *pages 12, 18, 41, 46, 49, 55, 62, 84.* Stacey Schuett *pages 10, 16, 24, 25.*

Technical Art: Taurins Design

Photos: Corbis *pages iv, 1, 2, 4, 6, 7, 8, 9, 15, 18, 19, 21, 22, 28, 30, 31, 36, 37 (top left & right), 47, 51, 54, 55, 58, 59, 63, 64, 66, 72, 73, 75, 76, 82, 90, 91 (top right), 92, 97, 98.* Walter M. Edwards/National Geographic Image Collection *page 37.* The Mariners' Museum, Newport News, VA *page 79.* Naives & Visionaries, Walker Art Center, E.P. Dutton & Co, 1974 *page 91 (top left).* Thos K. Meyer *page 91 (bottom right).* Virginia Kazor *pages 94, 95, 96, 101.*

Cover Design: Kristen Davis

Table of Contents

Chapter 1

Fantastic Flights
Reading Piece by Piece 1
 Understanding Common Words or Phrases 2
 Visualizing a Math Sentence 10
 Using Math Symbols 14
 Chapter Test 16

Chapter 2

Postcards from the States
Finding Exactly What You Need 18
 Finding Information You Need to Solve a Problem 20
 Problems with Missing Information 30
 Chapter Test 34

Chapter 3

Amazing Caves
Making a Plan 36
 Visualizing a Math Problem 38
 Making a Plan 46
 Chapter Test 52

Chapter 4

Fancy Feathers
Carrying Out the Plan 54
 Choosing the Correct Solution 56
 Using a Plan to Solve a Problem 62
 Writing the Plan and Solving the Problem 66
 Chapter Test 70

Chapter 5

Treasures from the Deep
Looking Back 72
 Answering the Question Asked 74
 Comparing Your Answer to Another Number 78
 Using the Correct Label for Your Answer 82
 Using Estimation to Check Your Answer 84
 Chapter Test 88

Chapter 6

A Towering Contest
Putting It All Together 90
 Using the Four-Step Problem-Solving Method 92
 Solving Math Problems on Your Own 102
 Chapter Test 106

Vocabulary 108

Chapter 1

Fantastic Flights
Reading Piece by Piece

Forever Rainbows Film Company

Dear _____,
        (Your Name)

We are planning a series of films on aviation. The series will be called *Fantastic Flights*. We want students to learn about some of the amazing airplanes, pilots, and important events in the history of aviation.

We would like to ask for your help on the making of the documentaries. We hope you will accept this exciting assignment. We look forward to hearing from you soon.

Sincerely,

Kyle Hart

Kyle Hart
President
Forever Rainbows Film Company

Dear Mr. Hart,

I would love to help you with this series of films on aviation. I can hardly wait to get started.

Sincerely,

_____
        (Your Name)

In this chapter, you will learn some *firsts* in aviation history. To fly an airplane, pilots need to make sure they understand correctly everything they read and see on the instrument panels. Just like a pilot, when reading a word problem, you need to pay special attention to math-related words, phrases, sentences, and symbols. You'll get lots of practice using the first step of the four-step problem solving method: **Understand.**

▲ Wilbur Wright watches as his brother, Orville, takes off in the *Wright Flyer* on December 17, 1903.

The Wright Brothers had a bicycle-making shop in Ohio in the early 1900s. They also dreamed of flying an airplane. Orville Wright was the pilot of the world's first airplane flight when he took off from a beach near Kitty Hawk, North Carolina.

Imagine it is a beautiful sunny day with a clear blue sky overhead. All of a sudden 6 jets streak by with white smoke trails streaming behind them. You are watching a performance of the *Blue Angels,* the famous precision formation flyers from the U.S. Navy and U.S. Marine Corps.

The *Blue Angels* began performing in 1946. Today they use 6 jets in their exciting air shows. More than 260 million people in the United States and around the world have watched the *Blue Angels* perform.

▲ Six *Blue Angel* jets flying in a Delta formation

Sometimes the same word can mean different things.

Sometimes one word can have different meanings. You can get an idea about its meaning by looking at how the word is used. For example, the word *right* is often used to describe position, as in the jet flies *right* wing.
Other times, the word can mean correct, as in the *right* answer.

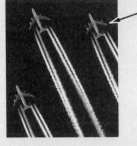

right wing

$$295$$
$$+ \ 140$$
$$\overline{435} \ \checkmark$$

right answer

There are many words with special math meanings that are not the same as the everyday meaning of the same words.

In front of exercises 1–2, write the letter of the picture that best shows the meaning of the underlined word.

These numbers tell you where to find more information in *Math to Know*.

_____ **1.** James Banning and Thomas Allen were the first black aviators to fly across the United States. Their flight took <u>under</u> 42 hours. ◀MTK 12

_____ **2.** The wheels of the airplane are <u>under</u> the body of the plane. ◀MTK 12

A.

Look for the vocabulary words on this page. Circle them, then go to the Vocabulary Section, which begins on page 108. Write a definition for the words. Include diagrams or examples.

B.

2   Vocabulary ▾ right ▾ under ▾ hour (h)

In front of exercises 3–4, write the letter of the picture that shows the meaning of the one word that completes both sentences. Write the word in the blank.

_____ **3.** One of the first passenger flights had an _____ number of passengers, 5, on board. ◀ MTK 91

_____ **4.** Flying upside down can give you an _____ feeling in your stomach.

A.

B.

In exercises 5–6, use the word <u>left</u> in a sentence that describes the picture. ◀ MTK 46

5.

Kitty Hawk
Keep Left

_____

_____

6.

_____

_____

more ▶

Vocabulary ▾ odd ▾ left

Sometimes a math word can have more than one math meaning.

You need to be clear about how you use math words. For example, the word *zero* has two different meanings in math. The word *zero* is the name for the symbol 0. The word *zero* also means empty or having no value.

There is a *zero* in the number 2605. ◄MTK 7

The plane has no fuel. The gauge is pointing to *EMPTY*.

In front of exercises 7–8, write the letter of the picture that best shows the meaning of the underlined word.

_____ **7.** The *Wright Flyer* traveled one <u>fourth</u> of the total distance on the ground. ◄MTK 210

> **Did you know?**
> On its first flight, the *Wright Flyer* went a total distance of 160 feet. It traveled 40 feet on the ground and flew 120 feet in the air.

_____ **8.** On the <u>fourth</u> of June in 1784, Madame Elisabeth Thible of Lyon, France became the first woman to fly a hot-air balloon. ◄MTK 16

A.

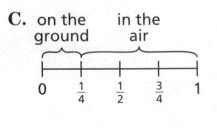

B.

June						
Mon.	Tues.	Wed.	Thurs.	Fri.	Sat.	Sun.
	1	2	3	④	5	6
7	8	9	10	11	12	13
14	15	16	17	18	19	20
21	22	23	24	25	26	27
28	29	30				

C. on the ground   in the air

$$0 \qquad \frac{1}{4} \qquad \frac{1}{2} \qquad \frac{3}{4} \qquad 1$$

Vocabulary ▼ zero ▼ fourth ▼ total ▼ first (*adj*) ▼ foot *or* feet (ft)

In front of exercises 9–10, write the letter of the picture that shows the meaning of the one word that completes both sentences. Write the word in the blank.

_____   9. It is 90 _____ Fahrenheit outside. ◀MTK 360

_____ 10. The drawing has a 90 _____ angle. ◀MTK 307

A.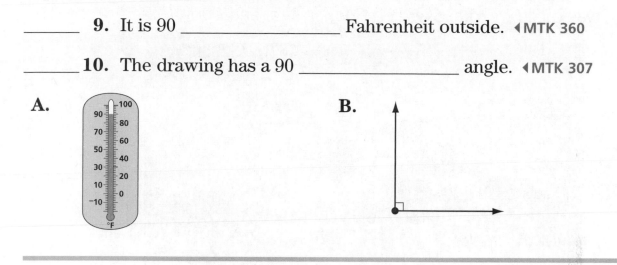

B.

For exercises 11–12, use the word <u>quarter</u> in a sentence that describes the picture.

11.      ◀MTK 17

_____

_____

12.   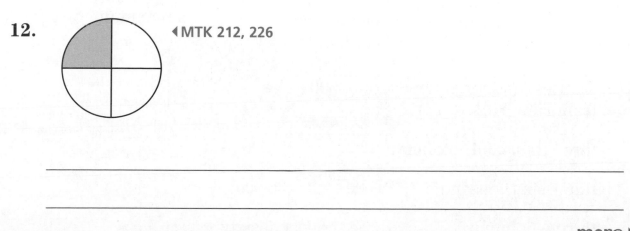   ◀MTK 212, 226

_____

_____

more ▶

Vocabulary ▾ degree (°) ▾ Fahrenheit (F) ▾ angle ▾ quarter

Sometimes different words can mean or name the same thing.

The DC-3 passenger airplane had many different names. It was called *Dakota*, *Skytrain*, *Gooney Bird*, and *Dizzy Three*.

In math, we also have different ways to name the same thing.

Circle the words or numbers that mean the same as the underlined part in the sentence. Circle as many as apply.

13. A pilot needs to have <u>at least 1500</u> hours of fighter pilot experience to join the *Blue Angels*. ◄ MTK 4, 5

no less than 1500	1500 or more	a minimum of 1500
less than 1500	1500 or less	a maximum of 1500

14. Charles Lindbergh flew about <u>3600</u> miles from New York to Paris, France. ◄ MTK 6–7

three thousand, six hundred

thirty-six thousand   3,600   36,000

thirty-six hundred   three thousand, sixty

> **Did you know?**
> Charles Lindbergh was the first to fly solo from New York to Paris, France. The name of his airplane was *The Spirit of St. Louis*.

Vocabulary ▾ less than (<) ▾ minimum ▾ maximum ▾ mile (mi) ▾ thousand ▾ hundred

15. One <u>third</u> of the *Blue Angel* jets are in the air. ◀MTK 210–213

third	$\frac{1}{3}$	13	one out of three
one	1	3	1 out of 3

16. Domingo Rosillo received a reward of <u>$10,000</u> for being the first person to fly from Florida to Cuba. ◀MTK 6–7, 17

ten thousand dollars   one thousand dollars

one hundred thousand dollars   one million dollars

For exercises 17–19, write another word or phrase that means the same as the underlined part of the sentence.

17. Amy Johnson's flight from England to Australia in 1930 took 19 days <u>in all</u>.

_____

_____

Amy Johnson was the first woman to fly solo from England to Australia.

18. Helen Richey held an altitude record for airplanes weighing <u>less than</u> 440 pounds. ◀MTK 12

_____

_____

Helen Richey was the first woman pilot hired by a commercial airline.

19. Today the *Blue Angels* fly <u>twice</u> as many jets in a performance as when they started.

_____

_____

more ▶

Vocabulary ▾ one third ▾ twice

S̲ome numbers tell exact amounts. Other numbers just tell *about* how many or *about* how much.

Look at the sentence below.

In 1963, Jacqueline Cochran set a world speed record for women pilots when she flew at about <u>1400</u> miles per hour.

In this sentence, the number 1963 is an exact number.

The number 1400 is a rounded number. It gives an estimate of the speed flown.

Jacqueline Cochran was the first woman to fly faster than the speed of sound.

Read the story. Underline the numbers you think are exact. Circle the numbers you think are estimates. ◄MTK128–130

20.

The airplane named the Jenny got its start in 1914. The Jenny had the best features of Model J and Model N. That is how it became known as the Jenny.

About 2600 models were made. The Jenny was $27\frac{1}{3}$ feet long with a wingspan of about 40 feet. It weighed about 1600 pounds and carried 26 gallons of fuel. The Jenny climbed close to 2000 feet in about 10 minutes. The fastest speed a Jenny flew was about 75 miles per hour with a crew of two.

The Jenny was often used in what were called barnstorming shows during the 1920s, which became known as *The Jenny Era*. People would climb out on the wing of a Jenny while it was flying and do stunts. Two men even played tennis on the wings of a Jenny. They stood about 30 feet apart with a net in between them.

Did you know?
Barnstorming came from a term used by traveling theater groups who performed in barns.

The Jenny was put on a United States postage stamp in 1918. The value of the stamp was 24¢. However, one sheet of exactly 100 stamps was printed with upside down Jennys on them. This stamp has since become known as the *Inverted Jenny*.

Today, just one of those stamps alone is worth over $100,000. So if you find a stamp with an upside down Jenny, don't throw it away!

Did you know?
The clerk at the post office who sold the sheet of *Inverted Jenny* stamps didn't know that the plane was upside down. He had never seen an airplane before!

Vocabulary ⬏ **pound (lb)** ⬏ **gallon (gal)** ⬏ **minute (min)** ⬏ **cent (¢)**

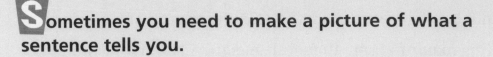
Sometimes you need to make a picture of what a sentence tells you.

To help you understand a math sentence, create a picture of what you see in your mind when you read the sentence.

What do you see when you read this sentence?

The 6 *Blue Angel* pilots shared the cake equally.

Here are two different ways you can picture the sentence.

You can draw a very realistic picture with lots of details. Or, you can draw a simple sketch to show the math.

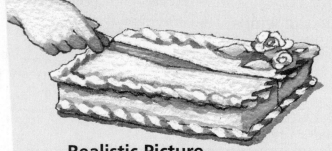

Realistic Picture   **Simple Sketch**

A simple sketch can help you pay attention to what's important. And, it also takes less time to draw.

In front of exercises 1–4, write the letter of the picture that best shows the meaning of the math.

_____ **1.** There were 3 airplanes, each with 2 pilots in it. ◀ MTK 64–65

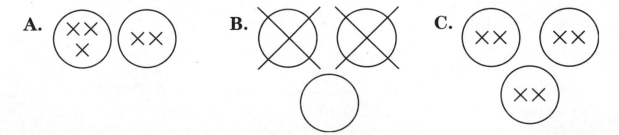

_____ **2.** The fuel tank was two-thirds full. ◂MTK 210-213

A.

B.

C.

_____ **3.** The wings of the 2 *Blue Angel* planes were 36 inches apart. ◂MTK 346

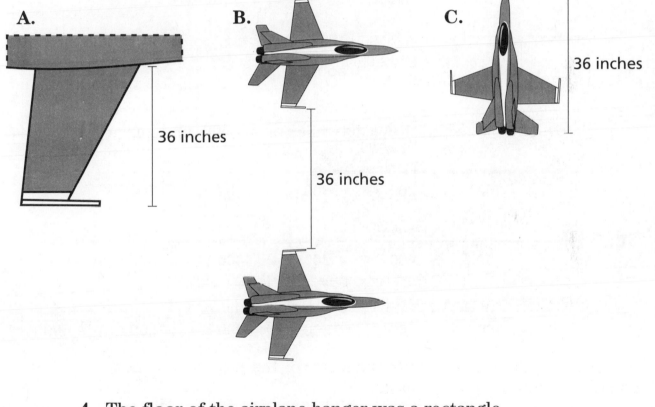

A.

36 inches

B.

36 inches

C.

36 inches

_____ **4.** The floor of the airplane hanger was a rectangle 60 feet long by 40 feet wide. ◂MTK 349

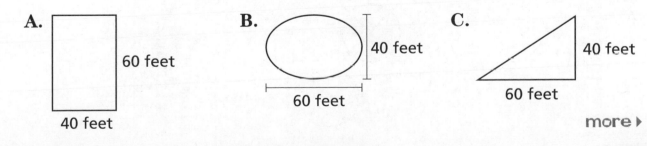

A.

60 feet

40 feet

B.

40 feet

60 feet

C.

40 feet

60 feet

more ▸

Vocabulary ▾ two thirds ▾ inch (in.) ▾ rectangle

Useful math pictures describe what is needed to solve a problem.

In front of exercises 5–7, write the letter of the picture that best shows the meaning of the math.

_____ **5.** The suitcase weighed 6 pounds. ◀MTK 358

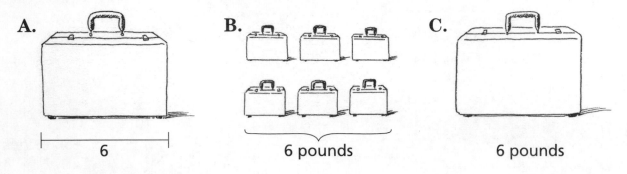

A.

6

B.

6 pounds

C.

6 pounds

_____ **6.** The plane had flown 300 miles of the 600-mile journey. ◀MTK 346

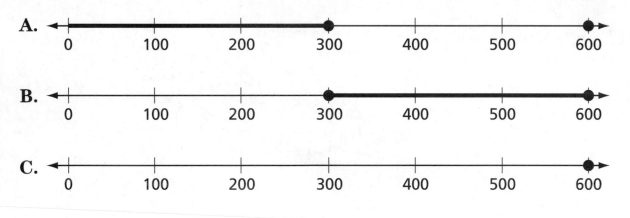

A.

0   100   200   300   400   500   600

B.

0   100   200   300   400   500   600

C.

0   100   200   300   400   500   600

_____ **7.** The temperature was 86 degrees Fahrenheit. ◀MTK 360

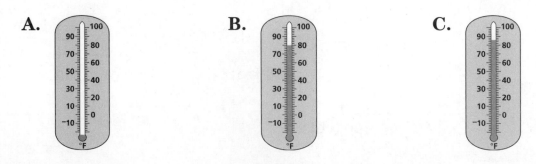

A.

B.

C.

Vocabulary ▼ temperature

Draw a picture to represent the sentence.

8. There were 5 hot air balloons with 3 people in each balloon basket. ◀MTK 64–65

9. The 6 *Blue Angel* pilots shared a pie equally. ◀MTK 210–211

10. The tray table for each seat in the airplane was 17 inches long and 12 inches wide. ◀MTK 349

11. One third of the 12 passengers were children. ◀MTK 214–215

Vocabulary ▬ long ▬ wide

Symbols can be used to stand for one word or a group of words.

Often on airport runways people are too far away or there is too much noise to talk. Pilots and the ground crew use signals to communicate. Each signal is a symbol with a special meaning.

Do Not Land Here Signal

Land Here Signal

Negative Signal

These signals replace words, so that messages can be understood when spoken or written words won't work.

In math, we often use symbols as a short cut to write a word or group of words.

Sometimes when you are solving a math problem, it helps if you can replace some of the words with a symbol.

Write one of the symbols from below in each ◯ so that the two sentences in each group are true. ◀MTK 12–13, 224–225, 471–472

$$+ \quad - \quad \times \quad \div \quad > \quad < \quad =$$

1. Chuck Yeager's new record of flying 956 miles per hour was faster than his earlier record of flying 760 miles per hour.

   a. Yeager's new record is ◯ his earlier record.

   b. Yeager's first record of flying 760 miles per hour is ◯ his later record of flying 956 miles per hour.

Chuck Yeager was the first person to fly faster than the speed of sound.

2. Richard Byrd's trip to the North Pole and back took $23\frac{1}{2}$ hours.

   Did you know?
   Richard Byrd and his team were the first to fly over the North Pole.

   a. The total number of hours for Byrd to get to the North Pole and back ◯ $23\frac{1}{2}$ hours

   b. The number of hours it took Byrd to get to the North Pole ◯ the number of hours it took Byrd to return from the North Pole ◯ $23\frac{1}{2}$ hours.

3. The Bessie Coleman stamp cost eight times as much as a 4¢ stamp.

   a. The cost of the Bessie Coleman stamp ◯ 8 ◯ the cost of a 4¢ stamp.

   b. 8 ◯ the cost of the 4¢ stamp ◯ the cost of the Bessie Coleman stamp.

Bessie Coleman was the world's first licensed black aviator. She was featured on a 32¢ stamp in the Black Heritage stamp series.

Vocabulary ▪ cost

15

Fill in the circle with the letter of the correct answer.

1. Which car has an odd number of people in it?

   (A) The blue car has 4 people in it.

   (B) The green car has 5 people in it.

   (C) The black car has 2 people in it.

2. Which cake is divided into fourths?

3. There were about 1000 people at the football game. A total of 756 hot dogs and 810 drinks were sold.

   In the sentence above, which number is an estimate?

   (A) 1000   (B) 756   (C) 812

4. The garden is a rectangle 8 feet long by 5 feet wide. Which picture below shows the garden?

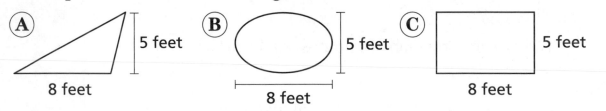

5. There are more apples than oranges in the bag. What is another way to write the sentence above?

   (A) The number of apples < the number of oranges.

   (B) The number of apples > the number of oranges.

   (C) The number of oranges > the number of apples.

Fill in the letter with the correct answer. Then write why you made that choice.

6. There were 4 cars, each with 3 people in them.

   Choose the picture that best shows the meaning of the sentence above.

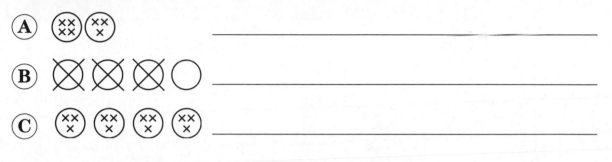

Answer the questions.

7. Explain, using words or pictures, two math meanings for the word <u>third</u>.

   • _____

   • _____

8. Draw a picture that represents the math in this sentence.

   The 8 cupcakes were divided into two even groups.

   Explain why your picture shows the math in the sentence.

   _____   **Draw your picture here.**

   _____

   _____

   _____

   _____

Chapter 2

Postcards From the States

Finding Exactly What You Need

18

In this chapter, you're a photographer collecting information and scenic photographs from all over the country to put on postcards. In your travels you'll come across all kinds of interesting data in paragraphs, tables, graphs, or diagrams. And you'll learn how to find just the information needed to solve a math problem. This will help you with the first step of the four-step problem-solving method: **Understand.**

◀ Rhode Island chose the violet as its state flower.

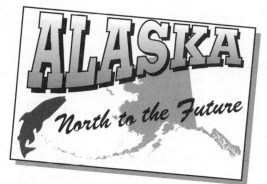

▲ Alaska's state motto is *North to the Future*.

▸ Dakota is the Sioux word for *friend*.

▼ The state flag of New Mexico has the ancient sun symbol of the Zia people.

▲ Delaware was the first to become a state of the United States and Hawaii was the 50th to become a state.

Information may be found in paragraphs, tables, graphs or diagrams.

You applied and got the job to create the postcards! Now you need to get started. With the help of some friends, you brainstorm a list of questions.

Do any of the state flags have animals on them?

Does each state have a state bird? How many states have the same state bird?

What do the new state quarters look like?

How was Mount Rushmore created?

How high is the highest point in Alabama?

How did the Statue of Liberty get to the United States from France?

You'll be finding the answers to these questions and many others as you do research for the postcards. You'll need to read very carefully so that you can find the exact information you need.

You decide to start the postcard series with state flags. For the state flag of Texas you see that it has 1 lone star on it. Curious, you wonder if other states have just 1 star on their flags as well. You also wonder if any state has exactly 1 animal on its flag. The Venn diagram shows the results of your research. ◀MTK 269

▲ State Flag of Texas

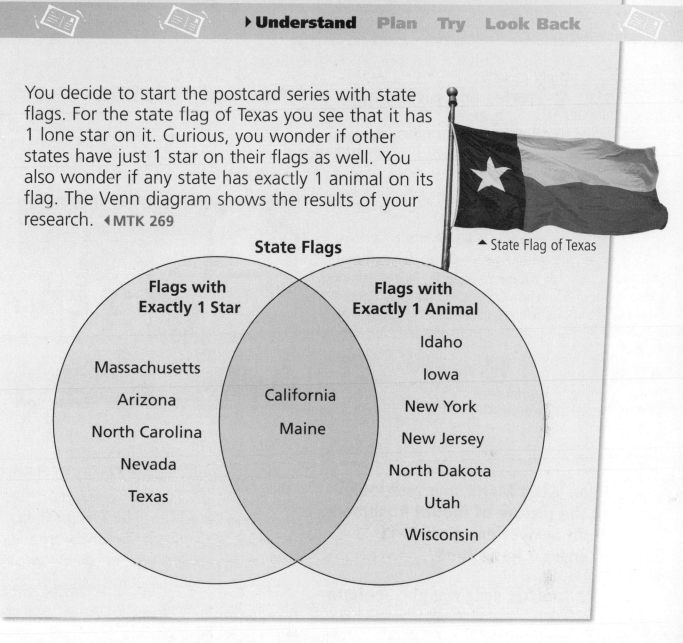

State Flags

| Flags with Exactly 1 Star | California Maine | Flags with Exactly 1 Animal |

Flags with Exactly 1 Star:
Massachusetts
Arizona
North Carolina
Nevada
Texas

(overlap): California, Maine

Flags with Exactly 1 Animal:
Idaho
Iowa
New York
New Jersey
North Dakota
Utah
Wisconsin

Use the information from the Venn diagram.
Write *True* or *False*. ◀MTK 269

_____ **1.** All states have exactly 1 star on their flags.

_____ **2.** California has exactly 1 star and exactly 1 animal on its flag.

_____ **3.** New York has exactly 1 animal on its flag.

_____ **4.** Maine is inside both circles.

_____ **5.** The diagram does not tell you about the flag of Nevada.

_____ **6.** Arizona is inside 1 circle only.

more ▶

Vocabulary ▼ Venn diagram

Stories and pictographs can show lots of information.

You decide to include Mount Rushmore in your postcard series. You travel to South Dakota. Maria Jimenez is a tour guide there. She talks about Mount Rushmore and how it was created.

The four presidents on Mount Rushmore are George Washington, Thomas Jefferson, Abraham Lincoln, and Theodore Roosevelt. Each face is about 60 feet high.

Did you know?
Gutzon Borglum was the sculptor who created Mount Rushmore.

60 feet

Read what Maria says and look at the picture of Mount Rushmore. Then answer exercises 7–11. Exercise 7 has a hint.

Gutzon Borglum began to sculpt Mount Rushmore in 1927 and finished in 1941. Close to 400 workers helped him. Over 450,000 tons of granite were removed by dynamite from the mountain during construction.

7. In what year was the sculpture completed? _____ ◀MTK 344

8. How much granite was removed from the mountain during construction? _____ ◀MTK 358

9. How many workers helped Borglum create the sculpture? _____

10. In what year did Borglum begin the sculpture? _____ ◀MTK 344

11. About how high is the face of each president? _____ ◀MTK 346

22   Vocabulary ▼ ton (t) ▼ high

You decide that some of your postcards will show state birds.

Popular State Birds

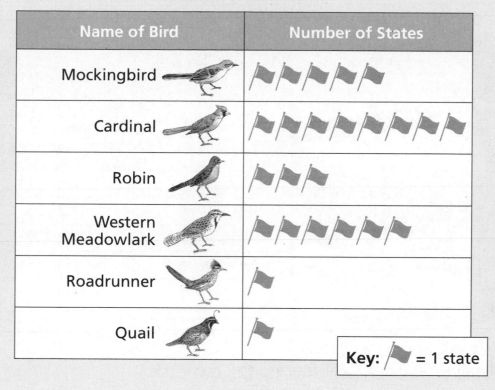

Name of Bird	Number of States
Mockingbird	(flags)
Cardinal	(flags)
Robin	(flags)
Western Meadowlark	(flags)
Roadrunner	(flag)
Quail	(flag)

Key: = 1 state

Use the pictograph to answer exercises 12–17. ◂MTK 270-271

12. How many states does each 🚩 stand for? _____

13. How many different kinds of birds are on the graph? _____

14. Which two birds appear the same number of times?

_____

15. Which bird is the second most popular? _____

16. What is the title of this pictograph? _____

17. To find the total number of each bird, do you count the

symbols in each row or in each column? _____

more ▸

Tables and bar graphs are also useful to display information.

You decide to design a postcard for each state with a cluster of photos from that state. On the backside you'll put the state's population data. ◄ MTK 266

State Population

State	Population
Alaska	626,932
Montana	902,195
North Dakota	642,200
South Dakota	754,844
Wyoming	493,782

Use the table to answer exercises 18–22. ◄ MTK 268

18. Which state in the table has the least population?

_____

19. Which state in the table has the greatest population?

_____

20. Name the state whose population is closest to half a million.

_____

21. Name the states listed with populations greater than 700,000.

_____

22. How many states in the table have a population

less than 400,000? _____

24   Vocabulary ▼ data ▼ least ▼ greatest ▼ million ▼ greater than (>)

Your friend, Karim, has a postcard collection from different states. He made a bar graph to display the postcards he has gathered from each state.

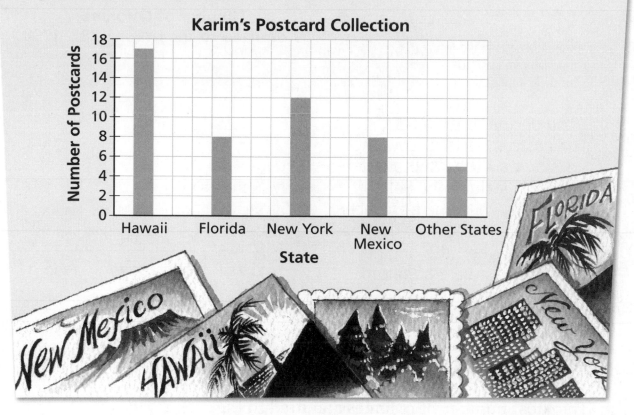

Use the bar graph to complete the sentences in exercises 23–28. ◀MTK 273

23. There are about _____twice_____ as many postcards from Hawaii as from Florida.

24. The number of postcards from _____ equals those from New Mexico.

25. Karim has 5 postcards from _____.

26. The number of postcards for _____ and _____ is the same.

27. There are more than 10 postcards from _____ states.

28. The second _____ postcards are from New York.

more ▶

Vocabulary ▼ bar graph ▼ equals (=) ▼ same ▼ second (*adj*)

Line plots show how data are clustered and line graphs show how data change over time.

The children in Massachusetts voted for the Minuteman statue for their state quarter.

You decide to do a set of postcards that shows the design on each state quarter. You will include the year each state became a member of the United States. The line plot tells when the original 13 colonies were admitted to the Union.

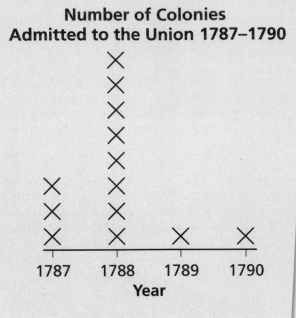

Number of Colonies Admitted to the Union 1787–1790

Use the line plot to answer exercises 29–33. ◄MTK 272

29. The most number of colonies admitted to the

   Union was in which year? _____

30. Were more colonies admitted to the Union in 1787 or 1790?

   _____

31. Which two years had the same number of colonies admitted

   to the Union? _____

32. In which years were at least 3 colonies admitted

   to the Union? _____

33. In which years were 2 or more colonies admitted to the Union?

   _____

Two photo shoots are planned for February. You will travel to Honolulu, Hawaii, and Minneapolis, Minnesota. To pack for each trip, you check out the temperature in February for both cities.

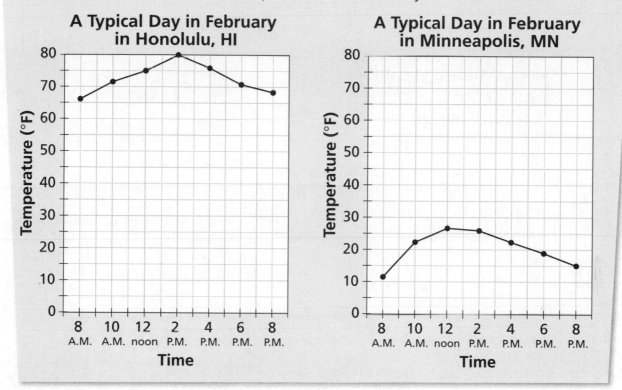

Use the line graphs to complete the sentences. ◂MTK 280–281

34. The temperature in Honolulu at 12 noon was _____ °F. ◂MTK 360

35. The temperature in Minncapolis at _____ was almost 20°F.

36. The highest temperature in Honolulu on the graph was _____ °F.

37. The lowest temperature in Minneapolis on the graph was a

little more than _____ °F

38. One piece of clothing suitable for Honolulu, but not Minneapolis,

is _____.

39. One piece of clothing suitable for Minneapolis, but not Honolulu,

is _____.

more ▸

Vocabulary ▾ A.M. ▾ P.M. ▾ line graph

Look at all the data and choose which facts to use.

You've got two more ideas. In one set of postcards, you'll put scenic photographs of the highest and lowest points in selected states. In another set you'll put photographs of state trees. Now you need to get the information.

Popular State Trees

Did you know?
The highest point in the United States is Mt. McKinley in Alaska, which rises 20,320 feet above sea level.

Highest and Lowest Points

State	Lowest Point		Highest Point	
Alabama	Gulf of Mexico Shoreline	0 feet	Cheaha Mountain	2,407 feet
Arkansas	Ouachita River	55 feet	Magazine Mountain	2,753 feet
Idaho	Snake River	710 feet	Borah Peak	12,662 feet
Maine	Atlantic Coast Shoreline	0 feet	Katahdin Mountain	5,268 feet
Michigan	Lake Erie Shoreline	572 feet	Mt. Arvon	1,980 feet
Minnesota	Lake Superior Shoreline	602 feet	Eagle Mountain	2,301 feet
Montana	Kootenai River	1,800 feet	Granite Peak	12,799 feet
North Carolina	Atlantic Coast Shoreline	0 feet	Mt. Mitchell	6,684 feet

DO NOT solve exercises 1–3. Instead, write the information you would use to solve the problem. Then circle where you found the information. ◂MTK 268, 273

40. Which is taller, Cheaha Mountain or Eagle Mountain?

To solve this problem, you need to find

a. the height of Cheaha Mountain: _____ 2,407 feet _____

b. the height of Eagle Mountain: _____

You got the information from the   bar graph   table

41. What is the difference between the lowest points in Montana and in Idaho?

To solve this problem, you need to find

a. the lowest point in Montana: _____

b. the lowest point in Idaho: _____

You got the information from the   bar graph   table

42. How many states have a maple, pine or oak tree as their state tree?

To solve this problem, you need to find

a. the number of states with a maple tree: _____

b. the number of states with a pine tree: _____

c. the number of states with an oak tree: _____

You got the information from the   bar graph   table

Vocabulary ▾ height ▾ difference

29

Sometimes a problem doesn't give you all the information you need.

To solve those problems, you may be able to find the missing information yourself. For example, you can use a reference book such as an almanac or encyclopedia. You might surf the Internet. Sometimes you can call a business or an organization to get more information.

The Statue of Liberty was a gift from the people of France and it was built there. A total of 350 individual pieces were put in 214 crates and shipped to the United States.

Read each problem. Then answer parts a and b.

1. To take a photograph of the Manhattan skyline from the crown on the Statue of Liberty, you climb the steps to the top. After 276 steps you stop for a rest. How many more steps are left to climb? ◄ MTK 5

   a. What information is missing from the problem?

   _____

   b. Can you find the missing information? If *yes*, write the information and tell how you found it.

   _____

2. The population of Vermont is 608,827. How many more people live in Alaska than in Vermont? ◄ MTK 9

   a. What information is missing from the problem?

   _____

   b. Can you find the missing information? If *yes*, write the information and tell how you found it.

   _____

30

The Space Needle is in Seattle, Washington.

3. The Space Needle is modeled after the Stuttgart Tower in Germany. The Space Needle is 605 feet tall. How much taller is the Stuttgart Tower than the Space Needle? ◀MTK 5

 a. What information is missing from the problem?

 _____

 b. Can you find the missing information? If *yes*, write the information and tell how you found it.

 _____

Half Dome rises over 4000 feet high.

4. You are going to photograph Half Dome in Yosemite. You have driven 163.5 kilometers. How much longer is the drive? ◀MTK 347

 a. What information is missing from the problem?

 _____

 b. Can you find the missing information? If *yes*, write the information and tell how you found it.

 _____

Did you know?
LeConte Memorial Lodge is Yosemite's visitor center and a National Historic Landmark.

5. The cost to mail a First Class letter and a large postcard is the same. Is 50¢ enough to buy a stamp to mail a large postcard of LeConte Memorial Lodge? ◀MTK 17

 a. What information is missing from the problem?

 _____

 b. Can you find the missing information? If *yes*, write the information and tell how you found it.

 _____

more ▶

Vocabulary ▼ kilometer (km)

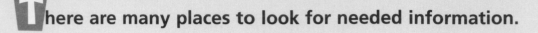

There are many places to look for needed information.

Read each problem. Then answer parts a and b.

6. What is the difference in feet between the highest and lowest points in Idaho? ◀MTK 345

    a. What information is missing from the problem?

    _____

    b. Can you find the missing information? If *yes*, write the information and tell how you found it.

    _____

7. There are 2 stores that sell your postcards. You've given 125 postcards to one of the stores. How many postcards have you given to both stores? ◀MTK 5

    a. What information is missing from the problem?

    _____

    b. Can you find the missing information? If *yes*, write the information and tell how you found it.

    _____

8. The postcard project is a success. Friends are coming over to celebrate. You decide to bake a chocolate cake. Is there enough time? ◀MTK 334

    a. What information is missing from the problem?

    _____

    b. Can you find the missing information? If *yes*, write the information and tell how you found it.

    _____

You have finished your postcard project and the postcards are selling very well. You've learned a lot about the states in the United States. Answer the following questions about some of the things you have learned.

Write the answer to each question. Then write the page number where you found that information.

9. What is the motto of the state of Alaska?

_____ (page _____)

10. What is the name of a state that has exactly 1 star and exactly 1 animal on its flag?

_____ (page _____)

11. Which four American presidents are represented on Mount Rushmore?

_____ (page _____)

12. Who decided what would go on the state quarter for Massachusetts?

_____ (page _____)

13. What is the highest point in the United States?

_____ (page _____)

14. The Statue of Liberty is a gift to the people of the United States from which European country?

_____ (page _____)

15. Where is the Space Needle located?

_____ (page _____)

16. What is the name of the visitor center in Yosemite National Park?

_____ (page _____)

Fill in the circle with the letter of the correct answer.

1. Look at the information in the table.

   According to the information, which sentence is *not* true?

   Zoo Visitors

Month	Adults	Children
January	1,256	1,875
February	1,349	2,403
March	2,650	2,798
April	2,976	3,011
May	2,756	2,901
June	3,659	4,002

   (A) In March 2,650 adults came to the zoo.

   (B) There were more adults who came to the zoo in February than in April.

   (C) In May 2,901 children came to the zoo.

   (D) There were more children who came to the zoo in June than in January.

2. Look at the information in the bar graph.
   On which days did Suki practice ice-skating more than 1 hour?

   Number of Hours Practicing Ice Skating

   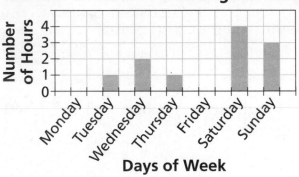

   Days of Week

   (A) Tuesday and Thursday

   (B) Monday, Tuesday, Thursday, and Friday

   (C) Wednesday, Saturday, and Sunday

   (D) Tuesday

Choose the letter of the best answer, then write why you made that choice.

3. Roberto gives Sam 32 baseball cards. How many baseball cards does Roberto have left?

   What information is needed to answer the problem?

   Ⓐ   the number of baseball cards Sam has in his collection

   _____

   Ⓑ   the date Roberto gave Sam the baseball cards

   _____

   Ⓒ   the number of players on a baseball team

   _____

   Ⓓ   the number of baseball cards Roberto started with

   _____

Use the information in the bar graph to answer question 4.

4. Write 4 things this bar graph tells you about Maria's postcard collection from different states.

   _____

   _____

   _____

   _____

   _____

   _____

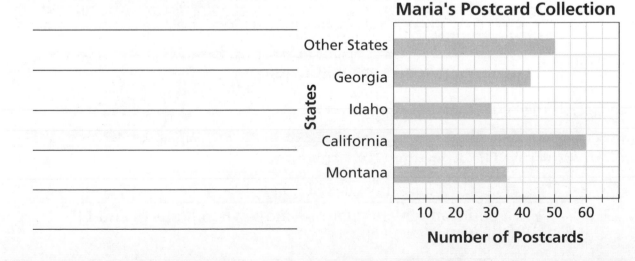

Maria's Postcard Collection

Chapter 3

Amazing Caves
Making a Plan

Send To / **Attachments**

TO

_____
(Your Name)

From: LupeSpelunker@AmazingCaves.com

subject : The Amazing Cave Adventure

I'm taking a group of students to visit famous caves all over the world. You are invited to join us on *The Amazing Cave Adventure*. Being a good problem solver is a very important skill to bring on a cave exploration. For example, before we leave on the trip, we have to figure out how much equipment and supplies to bring for the entire time. Once inside a cave, we won't come back out until the end of the journey.

On *The Amazing Cave Adventure*, we'll see some really incredible sights and run into all kinds of interesting problems to solve. Sound exciting? I hope you think so and that you'll join me on this one-of-a-kind experience.

Send To / **Attachments**

TO LupeSpelunker@AmazingCaves.com

From: _____
(Your Name)

subject : *re* The Amazing Cave Adventure

YES, count me in! Just let me know when it starts and I'll be there.

As you go on *The Amazing Cave Adventure*, you'll learn how making mental pictures and writing plans help people explore caves and solve math problems. You will get lots of practice using the first and second steps in the four-step problem-solving method: **Understand** and **Plan**.

▸ Four boys searching for their lost dog discovered Lascaux Cave in France in 1940. One of the boys, Jacques Marsal, became a guide for the caves as an adult. These caves are filled with paintings of wild horses, woolly mammoths, and other animals, all created between 30,000 and 10,000 BC.

◂ Mammoth Cave in Kentucky is the longest cave that we know of in the world. A hunter following a wounded bear discovered it in 1799.

▸ Stephen Bishop was a slave who explored Mammoth Cave. In 1842, he drew a map of the cave that was used for many years.

▾ Carlsbad Caverns in New Mexico was discovered in 1885. Jim White and his son thought they saw smoke coming from the spot, but discovered that it was millions of bats flying out the cavern opening.

Did you know?

In the 1880s a French lawyer named Edouard-Alfred Martel became the Father of Cave Exploration. Martel figured out how to find the height of a cave. He filled a balloon with hot air and tied a string to it. Then he let go of the balloon but held onto the string like a kite. When the balloon reached the roof of the cave, he pulled it back in, measured its length, and found the height for that part of the cave!

Sometimes it helps to make a picture of a problem.

What's it like to go into a cave for the first time?

Would you feel excited, nervous, or scared?

For each trip, cavers always bring along a good drawing of the cave. It helps them know what to expect and to plan for a safe journey.

Many drawings have been made of the caves in Carlsbad Caverns. This chart shows a drawing, what it means, and how the drawing helps cavers plan their journeys through the caverns.

Drawing	Meaning	Plan
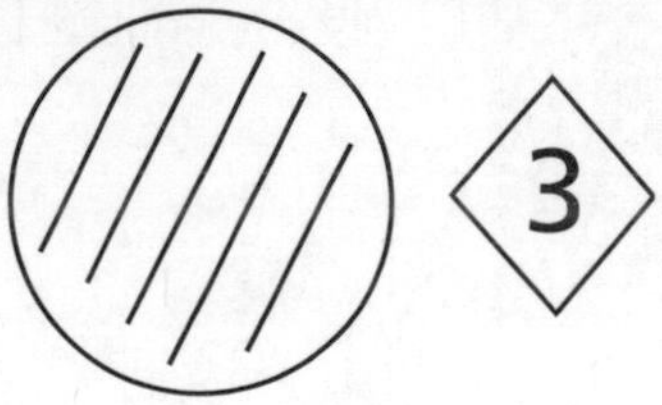	pool, 3 feet deep	Walk around the pool.
	breakdown wall	Watch for falling rocks.
	stream	Protect feet from cold water.

There are about 17,000 known caves in the United States. Many are located where Tennessee, Alabama, and Georgia meet.

Before starting out, always check to make sure you have the equipment needed. Here is your first problem:

> **Each of the 4 people in your group needs 3 flashlights. If one flashlight goes out, there are two more for back up. How many flashlights does your group need?**

When you read a math problem, it helps to make a mental picture of the problem. You can imagine 4 people, each with 3 flashlights.

Or, you can draw a simple picture to show 4 groups, each with 3 ×s for flashlights.

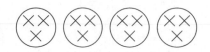

Both pictures help you see that you multiply to find the answer. ◀ MTK 64–65

$$4 \times 3 = 12$$

So, make sure there are 12 flashlights. Now you're set to roll.

Here is a surprise—*The Amazing Cave Adventure* has a cool travel machine that transports you instantly from one cave to another, anywhere in the world. Close your eyes, think hard about Lascaux Cave, and off you go!

Read the problem. Then follow the directions.

1. *Zap!* You are in the Lascaux Cave in France. You walk 66 feet from the entrance to the *Hall of Bulls* and then another 98 feet to the *Painted Gallery*. How far have you walked? ◀ MTK 250, 346

Circle the picture that shows the problem.

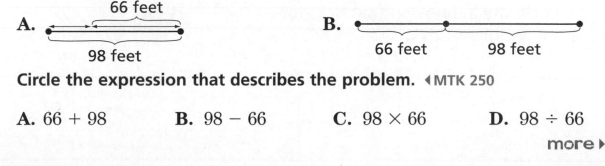

Circle the expression that describes the problem. ◀ MTK 250

A. $66 + 98$ **B.** $98 - 66$ **C.** 98×66 **D.** $98 \div 66$

more ▶

Vocabulary ▾ expression

39

A good math picture can help you decide how to solve a problem.

Read each problem. Then follow the directions.

2. *Swoosh!* You are at the natural opening of the Wind Cave in South Dakota. The diameter of the opening is 10 inches. What is the radius? ◀MTK 316

   Circle the picture that shows the problem.

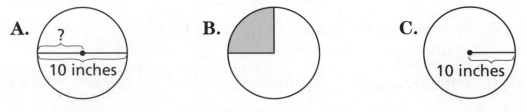

   Circle the expression that describes the problem.

   A. 10 + 2   **B.** 10 − 2   **C.** 10 × 2   **D.** 10 ÷ 2

3. Did you know that $\frac{1}{4}$ of the caves in the United States that are open to the public are in state parks? What fraction of the caves that are open to the public are *not* in state parks? ◀MTK 232

   Circle the picture that shows the problem.

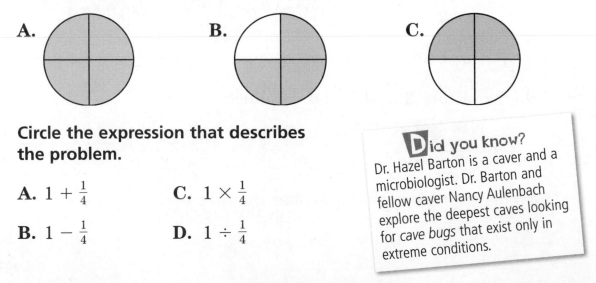

   Circle the expression that describes the problem.

   A. $1 + \frac{1}{4}$ **C.** $1 \times \frac{1}{4}$

   B. $1 - \frac{1}{4}$ **D.** $1 \div \frac{1}{4}$

   Did you know?
   Dr. Hazel Barton is a caver and a microbiologist. Dr. Barton and fellow caver Nancy Aulenbach explore the deepest caves looking for cave *bugs* that exist only in extreme conditions.

Vocabulary ▾ diameter (*d*) ▾ radius (*r*) ▾ fraction

4. *Zap!* You're at Carlsbad Caverns National Park. Bats live in the caves here. On average, about 300 bats live in one square foot. How many bats live in 4 square feet on average? ◂MTK 172-173, 284, 350-351

> **D**id you know?
> Bats have very poor vision, so they use echolocation to *see*. They send out sounds to bounce off objects. The time it takes for the echo to bounce back tells a bat how far away something is, its size and shape. This is how they catch mosquitoes!

Circle the picture that shows the problem.

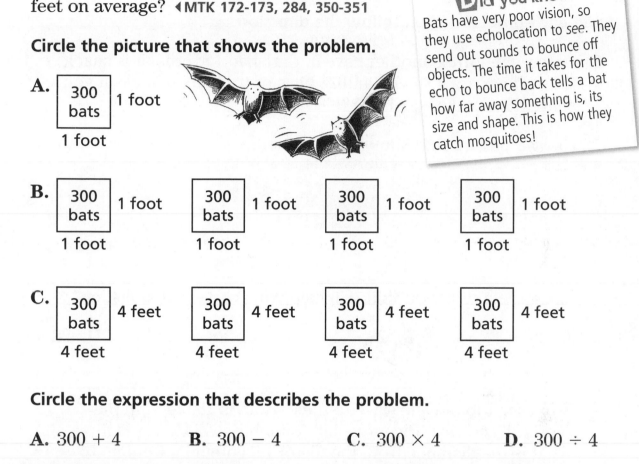

Circle the expression that describes the problem.

A. $300 + 4$ **B.** $300 - 4$ **C.** 300×4 **D.** $300 \div 4$

5. One bat is 3 feet from a column in a cave. Another bat is 5 feet from the same column. How much closer to the column is the first bat? ◂MTK 52

Circle the picture that shows the problem.

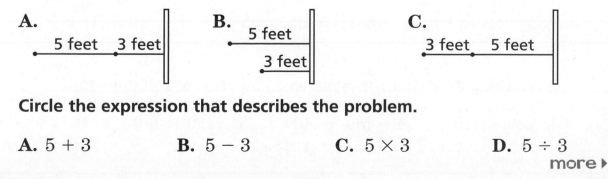

Circle the expression that describes the problem.

A. $5 + 3$ **B.** $5 - 3$ **C.** 5×3 **D.** $5 \div 3$

more ▸

Vocabulary ▾ average ▾ square foot *or* feet (ft²)

Read each problem. Then follow the directions.

6. Before exploring another cave in Carlsbad Caverns, it is snack time. There are 4 of you and 28 bags of trail mix. How can you share the snacks equally? ◀MTK 78–79

   Draw a picture that shows the problem.

   Circle the expression that will help you answer the question.

   A. $28 + 4$ **B.** $28 - 4$ **C.** 28×4 **D.** $28 \div 4$

---

7. From the top of Ogle Cave to the bottom is 180 feet. In the center of the cave Bicentennial Column rises 110 feet high. What is the distance from the top of Bicentennial Column to the ceiling of the Ogle Cave? ◀MTK 52

   Draw a picture that shows the problem.

   Circle the expression that will help you answer the question.

   A. $180 + 110$ **B.** $180 - 110$ **C.** 180×110 **D.** $180 \div 110$

Use a simpler problem to plan your solution.

You can change the numbers in a problem to make it easier to plan a solution. Then, go back and solve the original problem.

Example
Original problem On Monday, Carlsbad Caverns had 1,402 visitors and then 1,376 on Tuesday. How many people visited in all? ◀MTK 146–147

Think!

Simpler problem There were 3 visitors on Monday and 5 visitors on Tuesday. How many visitors were there in all?

Picture the simpler problem

Monday → 3
Tuesday → 5

How to solve simpler problem Visitors in all = Monday + Tuesday

How to solve original problem Add to find the sum: 1,402 + 1,376. ◀MTK 34–35

Think of a simpler problem first.

8. Neff Canyon Cave is 1,189 feet deep and Carlsbad Cavern is 1,022 feet deep. What is the difference in their depths? ◀MTK 50–53

Think!

Simpler problem One cave is 20 feet deep and another is 10 feet deep. What is the difference in their depths?

Picture the simpler problem

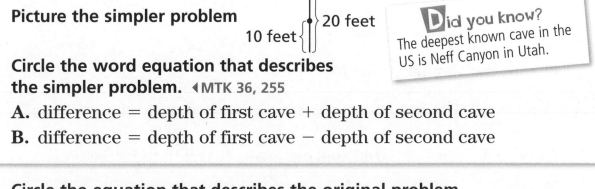

10 feet { | } 20 feet

> **Did you know?**
> The deepest known cave in the US is Neff Canyon in Utah.

Circle the word equation that describes the simpler problem. ◀MTK 36, 255

A. difference = depth of first cave + depth of second cave

B. difference = depth of first cave − depth of second cave

Circle the equation that describes the original problem.

A. difference = 1,189 + 1,022   **B.** difference = 1,189 − 1,022

more ▶

Vocabulary ⬝ sum ⬝ equation

Read each problem. Then follow the directions.

9. A ton equals 2,000 pounds. Iceberg Rock weighs 200,000 tons. How many pounds is that? ◀ MTK 36, 172–173

Think!

Simpler problem A ton equals 2,000 pounds. A rock weighs 3 tons. How many pounds is that?

Picture the simpler problem

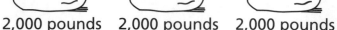

2,000 pounds   2,000 pounds   2,000 pounds

Circle the word equation that describes the simpler problem.

A. rock in pounds = 2,000 pounds × number of tons

B. rock in pounds = 2,000 pounds ÷ number of tons

Circle the equation that describes the original problem.

A. Iceberg Rock in pounds = 2,000 pounds × 200,000

B. Iceberg Rock in pounds = 2,000 pounds ÷ 200,000

---

10. The highest point in the Big Room in Carlsbad Caverns is about 255 feet. About how many acrobats, each 5 feet tall, would be needed to stand on each other's heads in order to reach the highest point? ◀ MTK 186–187

Think!

Simpler problem The height of a room is 15 feet. How many people who are 5 feet tall would be needed to stand on each other's heads in order to reach the ceiling?

⎫
⎬ 5 feet
⎭

⎫
⎬ 5 feet
⎭

⎫
⎬ 5 feet
⎭

Picture the simpler problem

Complete the word equation that describes the simpler problem.

people needed = height of _____ ÷ height of one _____

Circle the equation that describes the original problem.

A. people needed = 255 + 5   **B.** people needed = 255 ÷ 5

44

11. Lascaux Cave was discovered in 1940. Because of pollution and damage, they were closed to the public in 1963. How many years were the caves open to the public? ◂MTK 52

Think!

Write a simpler problem. _____

_____

Draw a picture of the simpler problem.

Write a word equation that describes the simpler problem.

_____

Circle the equation that describes the original problem.

A. years open = 1963 + 1940   **B.** years open = 1963 − 1940

12. One day there were 1,082 visitors to the Lascaux Caves. The next day there were 2,113. What was the difference in the number of visitors these two days? ◂MTK 160–165

Think!

Write a simpler problem. _____

_____

Draw a picture of the simpler problem.

Write a word equation that describes the simpler problem.

_____

Circle the equation that describes the original problem.

A. difference = 2,113 + 1,082   **B.** difference = 2,113 − 1,082

To solve a word problem, you need a plan that works.

It is very important to think ahead before you go into a cave.

What if you get to the cavern and find that your rope is too short?

What if your flashlight gives out and you don't have another battery?

What if you run out of food?

A caver needs to plan so that each trip is safe and successful.

Making a plan also helps when you solve a math problem. Some plans have one step, other times they have more than one step.

However, even the best-laid plans don't always work the way you think they should. You might get an answer that doesn't make any sense. When that happens, go back and try another plan.

Circle the plan that you could use to solve the problem.

1. Mammoth Cave is about 355 miles long. Jewel Cave is 119 miles long. Lechuguilla Cave is 101 miles long. How many miles would you walk if you walked the length of these three caves? ◄MTK 153, 346

Plan A

- Add 355 and 119 and 101.

- The answer will be in miles.

Plan B

- Add 355 and 119 and 101.

- The answer will be in square miles. ◄MTK 350

Did you know?
The three longest caves in the U. S. are Mammoth Cave in Kentucky, Jewel Cave in South Dakota, and Lechuguilla Cave in New Mexico.

46   Vocabulary ▼ length ▼ square mile (mi²)

2. *Flash!* You're at Cosquer Cave in France. To reach the cave you must first drop 125 feet below the water line and then go 575 feet along an underwater tunnel to get to the cave. If you have traveled 100 feet below the water line. How much further do you have to go before reaching the underwater tunnel? ◀MTK 146–152, 159–165

Plan A

- Add 125 and 575.
- The answer will be in feet.

Plan B

- Subtract 100 from 125.
- The answer will be in feet.

> **D**id you know?
> Cosquer Cave is an underwater cave discovered in 1985 in France. It has wall paintings of land animals and human handprints from 27,000 to 19,000 years ago.

3. To date, about 125 images of animals and 55 stenciled handprints have been found in Cosquer Cave. The stenciled handprints are what fraction of the total number of images? ◀MTK 210–216

Plan A Write a fraction.
- Find the total number of images.
- Use the total number of images as the numerator.
- Use 55 as the denominator.
- Simplify the fraction.

Plan B Write a fraction.
- Find the total number of images.
- Use 55 as the numerator.
- Use the total number of images as the denominator.
- Simplify the fraction.

more ▶

Vocabulary ▾ numerator ▾ denominator ▾ simplify

Having the right information can help you make a plan that works.

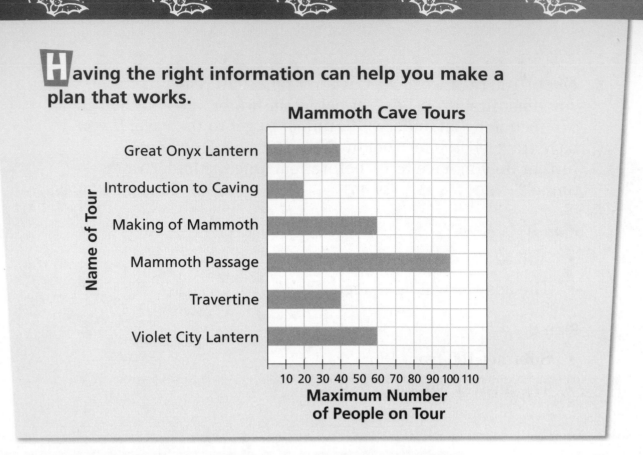

Mammoth Cave Tours

For exercises 4–6, use the information from the bar graph.
Circle the plan that you could use to solve the problem.

4. *Swoosh!* You are back in Kentucky, ready to tour Mammoth Cave. Both of the Lantern tours are sold out. How many people are on these 2 tours? ◀MTK 273, 146–147

    Plan A
    • Add 40 and 60.

    Plan B
    • Multiply 40 by 60.

5. What is the difference between the number of people on the Mammoth Passage tour as compared with those on the Introduction to Caving tour? ◀MTK 273, 159–160

    Plan A
    • Divide 20 by 100.

    Plan B
    • Subtract 20 from 100.

6. By 8 A.M., 28 people bought tickets for the Travertine tour. How many tickets are still available? ◀MTK 161, 273

    Plan A
    • Subtract 28 from 60.

    Plan B
    • Subtract 28 from 40.

Completing a plan can help you write one of your own.

Complete each plan. Fill in the blanks with a word from the box.

7. Some passengers on the Wild Cave tour measure no more than $3\frac{1}{2}$ feet around. How many inches is that? ◀MTK 172–181

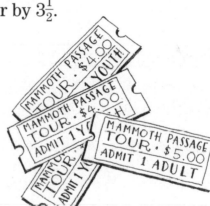

multiply
divide
inches ✔
foot
yard

Plan

- Find the number of __inches__ in one _____.

- _____ that answer by $3\frac{1}{2}$.

8. Mammoth Passage tour ticket for an adult costs $5 and a youth ticket costs $4. How much will it cost for 1 adult ticket and 3 youth tickets? ◀MTK 146–151, 172–181

add
subtract
multiply
divide
product
sum

Plan

- _____ $4 by 3.

- _____ $5 to the _____.

9. There are more than 250 cave entrances at Mammoth Cave National Park. However, only 30 lead directly to Mammoth Cave. What fraction of the entrances lead to the cave? ◀MTK 210–211

add
subtract
multiply
divide
numerator
denominator
fraction

Plan

- Write 30 in the _____.

- Write 250 in the _____.

- Write the _____ in lowest terms.   more ▶

Vocabulary ▾ measurement ▾ product

Write a plan for solving each problem.

10. Big Room in Carlsbad Cavern is a huge
    cave. Its entire floor area is over 300,000
    square feet. A football field is equal to
    a little over 57,000 square feet. So, about
    how many football fields can fit inside
    Big Room? ◄MTK 140, 184–206

    Plan

    • _____

    • _____

    • _____

> **D**id you know?
> One of the great attractions at
> Carlsbad Cavern is the *bat spectacle*.
> Each evening at dusk, except during
> the winter, millions of bats stream
> out from a cave 180 feet below the
> surface in search of food.

11. Big Room is nearly 4,000 feet long. Its maximum width is
    about 625 feet. At its highest, the ceiling rises to a height of
    350 feet. If Big Room were a prism, what would its volume
    be in cubic feet? ◄MTK 328, 354–355

    Plan

    • _____

    • _____

    • _____

12. One evening it took 2.75 hours for all the bats to leave the cave.
    The next evening it took 3.25 hours. How much longer did it
    take the second evening for all the bats to fly out? ◄MTK 168

    Plan

    • _____

    • _____

    • _____

Vocabulary ▾ width ▾ volume (*V*) ▾ prism ▾ cubic feet (ft³)

Great news! You have been invited to bring a group of cavers to explore a newly discovered cave. This means that you will be the second group of people to enter the cave.

You invite five caving friends and begin to plan for the trip.

13. The first thing to check is whether everyone has flashlights. You remember that each caver should carry 3 flashlights in case one is not enough. If each flashlight needs 3 size D batteries, will 30 batteries be enough? ◂MTK 60–66

Plan

- _____

- _____

- _____

14. There is a giant stalactite inside a room in the new cave. The room entrance is 3 miles from the cave opening. The stalactite is another 2 miles down a narrow passageway. How many miles is the round trip distance from the cave opening to the stalactite and back out again? ◂MTK 38-39

Plan

- _____

- _____

- _____

Your good planning has paid off. You've come out of the cave successfully and are ready to tell the world all about your amazing cave adventure.

Remember, if you make and follow a good plan, you will be successful in solving math problems.

A stalactite is a formation that hangs down from the ceiling of a cave.

Fill in the circle with the letter of the correct answer.

1. The fruit basket has 34 apples. Jose throws out two rotten apples. Which picture could you use to find the number of apples that are left?

Ⓐ   Ⓑ   Ⓒ

2. There are 3 people. Each person buys 5 raffle tickets. Which picture could you use to find the number of tickets they buy between them?

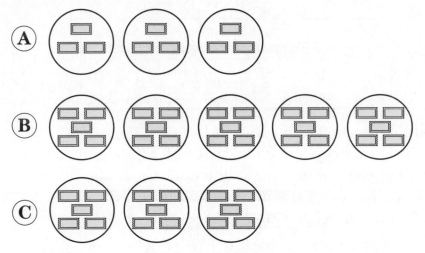

Ⓐ

Ⓑ

Ⓒ

3. Janet has 29 baseball cards. Doug gives her 18 baseball cards. Which picture could you use to find the number of baseball cards that Janet has now?

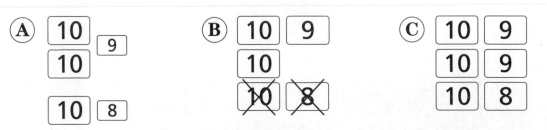

Ⓐ 10   9   Ⓑ 10   9   Ⓒ 10   9
    10   10   10   9
    10   8   10   8   10   8

4. Five people share 25 bus tokens equally. Which picture could you use to find the number of tokens each person gets?

Ⓐ   Ⓑ   Ⓒ

Fill in the circle with the letter of the correct answer. Write the reason why you made your choice.

5. Mrs. Lee pays $18 for 3 boxes of blank CDs. Each box costs the same. Which expression tells you how to find the cost of each box?

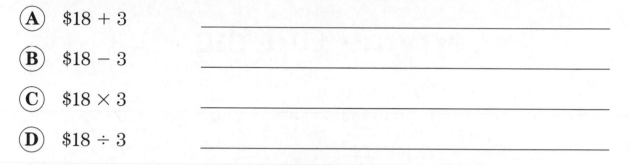

(A) $18 + 3   _____

(B) $18 − 3   _____

(C) $18 × 3   _____

(D) $18 ÷ 3   _____

For questions 6–8, write your answer on the lines provided.

6. The recipe calls for mixing $\frac{3}{4}$ cup of flour at the start and $\frac{1}{4}$ cup at the end. Tell what you would do to find the number of cups used.

_____

_____

7. You know there are 12 inches in a foot. The poster is 4 feet wide. Tell how to find the width in inches.

_____

_____

8. Write a math problem that could be solved using this plan.
   Plan
   • Add 25 and 35.
   • Subtract the sum from 98.

_____

_____

_____

Chapter 4

Fancy Feathers

Carrying Out the Plan

YOU ARE INVITED
TO JOIN

THE
FANCY FEATHERS
BIRD WATCHING
CLUB

We are a group of people
who travel all over the world
to see different kinds of birds.

To join, just send us a note.
Tell us the name of your favorite bird
and why you find it most interesting.

When you join the Fancy Feathers Bird Watching Club, you will travel all over the world to find interesting birds. To do that, you will need to have a plan for each trip. In this chapter, you will be making plans to solve word problems. You'll practice using the second and third steps of the four-step problem solving method: **Plan** and **Try**.

Many of the birds you will learn about in this chapter are featured on this page.

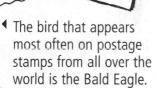

◄ The bird that appears most often on postage stamps from all over the world is the Bald Eagle.

▲ The earliest known flying bird is the Archaeopteryx. A fossilized feather from this bird was found in a piece of limestone believed to be about 145 million years old. Later, a complete skeleton of the feather was found. In Latin, the word *archaeopteryx* means *ancient feather* or *ancient wing*.

▸ Only the Emperor Penguins and one other species live in the ice and snow of the Antarctic.

▸ Airspace above two thirds of Bonaire Island is off-limits to planes. Only flamingos are allowed to fly in that space.

▲ If you stand near a Hummingbird, you can hear its wings making a whirring, or *humming*, sound. And, that is how the bird got its name.

55

Sometimes drawing a diagram can help you visualize your plan.

Start learning about birds right in your own backyard or on the street where you live. You'll need to be very still and quiet so as not to disturb the birds.

Birds love to bathe in shallow water. Putting in a birdbath will invite lots of birds to your backyard.

Solve the problems. The first exercise is done for you.

1. The shape of the birdbath is round. Its radius is 7 inches. What is the diameter? ◄MTK 316

Plan Fill in the blanks.

Think! • Draw a _____circle_____ with a diameter passing through the center.

• The diameter is _____two_____ times the radius.

• _____Multiply_____ 7 by ___2___.

• The unit in the answer will be _____inches_____.

Try Circle the diagram that fits the plan.

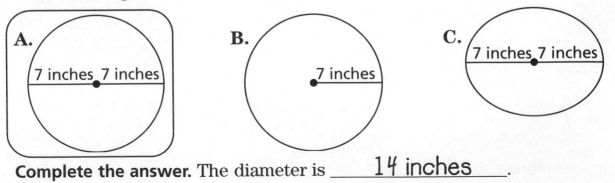

A. 7 inches 7 inches

B. 7 inches

C. 7 inches 7 inches

Complete the answer. The diameter is _____14 inches_____.

2. The birdbath is in the middle of a rectangular flowerbed that measures 8 feet by 6 feet. You want to build a foot path around the flowerbed. What is the perimeter of the flowerbed? ◂MTK 311, 348–349

Plan Fill in the blanks.

Think! • The flowerbed measures _____ feet by _____ feet.

• Find the sum of _____ + _____ + _____ + _____.

• The units in the answer will be _____.

Try Circle the diagram that fits the plan.

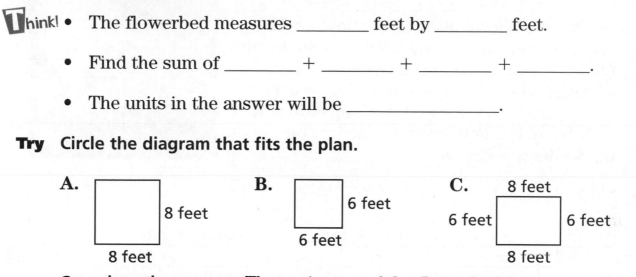

A. 8 feet, 8 feet

B. 6 feet, 6 feet

C. 8 feet, 6 feet, 6 feet, 8 feet

Complete the answer. The perimeter of the flowerbed is _____ feet.

---

3. You want to plant wildflowers in the flowerbed with the birdbath. What is the area of the flowerbed? ◂MTK 350–351

Plan Fill in the blanks.

Think! • Area measures the number of square units inside a _____.

• Draw a diagram that is _____ squares wide by _____ squares tall.

• Add the number of _____ in each row.

• The unit in the answer will be square _____.

Try Circle the work that fits the plan.

A. $8 + 8 + 8 + 8 + 8 + 8 = 48$

B. $6 + 6 + 6 + 6 + 6 + 6 = 36$

C. $8 + 6 = 14$

Complete the answer. The area is _____ square feet.

more ▸

Vocabulary ▾ perimeter (*P*) ▾ side ▾ area (*A*)

When carrying out your plan, it's important to check that you use the correct information.

Solve the problems.

4. Hummingbirds eat nectar from flowers. To provide sweet water feed for one hummingbird feeder you mix $\frac{1}{4}$ cup of sugar with 1 quart of water. There are 3 hummingbird feeders in the yard. How many cups of sugar do you need to make enough sweet water to fill the feeders? ◄MTK 228

Plan Fill in the blanks.

- The sweet water recipe calls for _____ cup of sugar.

- _____ to find the amount of sugar you need for 3 feeders.

- _____ + _____ + _____

- The unit in the answer will be _____.

Try Draw the diagram that fits the plan.

Circle the work that fits the plan.

A. $\frac{1}{4}$ cup + 1 quart = 1 quart $\frac{1}{4}$ cup

B. $\frac{1}{4}$ cup + $\frac{1}{4}$ cup + $\frac{1}{4}$ cup = $\frac{3}{4}$ cup

C. $\frac{1}{4}$ cup + $\frac{1}{4}$ cup + $\frac{1}{4}$ cup + 1 quart = 1 quart $\frac{3}{4}$ cup

Complete the answer. You need _____ cup of sugar.

Vocabulary ▾ cup (c) ▾ quart (qt)

5. You buy 2 guidebooks on birds native to your area. One costs $5.99 and the other $9.50. The sales tax for the purchase is $0.77. You give the cashier a $20 bill. How much change do you receive back? ◂MTK 20, 58, 171

Plan Fill in the blanks.

- Add _____, _____, and _____.

- _____ the sum from $20.

- The unit in the answer will be _____.

Try Draw the diagram that fits the plan.

Circle the pair of computations that fits the plan.

A.		**B.**		**C.**	
$20.00	$36.26	$5.99	$20.00	$5.99	$20.00
$9.50	−$20.00	$9.50	−$16.26	+$9.50	−$15.49
$5.99	$16.26	+$0.77	$3.74	$15.49	$35.49
+$0.77		$16.26			
$36.26					

Complete the answer. You receive _____ back in change.

more ▸

Vocabulary ▾ change

Solve the problems.

6. You decide to count birds in your backyard. One day you count 7 crows and 3 robins. The next day you count 5 crows and 6 robins. How many fewer robins than crows did you count on those two days? ◂MTK 36–37

Plan Fill in the blanks.

- _____ to find the number of crows.

- _____ to find the number of robins.

- _____ the number of robins from the number of crows.

- The answer tells the _____ between the number of robins and crows.

Try Draw the diagram that fits the plan.

Circle the three computations that fit the plan.

A.	7	3	12	**B.**	7	3	12	**C.**	7	3	12
	$+5$	$+6$	$+9$		$+5$	$+6$	-9		$+5$	$+6$	-9
	12	9	21		12	9	3		12	9	13

Complete the answer. You counted _____ fewer robins than crows.

2003 Great Backyard Bird Count Top 5 Sightings

1. American Goldfinch		2981
2. Northern Cardinal		2451
3. American Robin		2269
4. Mourning Dove		2118
5. Common Grackle		2019

7. The five most sighted birds in Alabama are shown in the table. If 500 more Common Grackles were sighted, where would that put it in the top five? ◂MTK 14–15

Plan **Fill in the blanks.**

- The bird count for the Common Grackle is _____ .

- _____ 500 to _____ .

- Compare the new sum to the other bird counts in the table.

Try **Compare the numbers. Use the table.**
The new sum for the Common Grackle is _____ .

The new sum is _____ than the number of sightings for the American Goldfinch.

The new sum is _____ than the number of sightings for the Northern Cardinal.

The new sum is _____ than the number of sightings for the American Robin.

The new sum is _____ than the number of sightings for the Mourning Dove.

List the numbers from greatest to least.

	Name of bird	Number
First place	_____	_____
Second place	_____	_____
Third place	_____	_____
Fourth place	_____	_____
Fifth place	_____	_____

Complete the answer. The Common Grackle in now in _____ place.

After you write a plan, it is important to try it out.

You decide to learn about different birds from around the world.

Read each problem. Then follow the directions.

1. The Blackpoll Warbler flies faster at the end of its migration than at the start. It sets out at about 30 miles daily. By the end, it flies about 200 miles a day. About how many more miles does the bird fly by the end of its migration? ◂MTK 160

Plan Fill in the blanks.

• _____ 30 from _____.

• The unit in the answer will be _____.

Try Use a drawing or compute to show your work.
Write your answer as a complete sentence.

_____

2. A hummingbird's wings beat about 234 times in 3 seconds. About how many times do the wings beat in 1 second? ◂MTK 186–189

Plan Fill in the blanks.

• _____ 234 by _____.

• The unit in the answer will be

beats per _____.

Try Use a drawing or compute to show your work.
Write your answer as a complete sentence.

_____

Bonaire Island

3. You travel to Bonaire Island to see the pink flamingos. To protect the flamingos, airplanes are not allowed to fly over $\frac{2}{3}$ of the island. What fraction of the air space above the island can airplanes fly over? ◂MTK 232

Plan Fill in the blanks.

Think! • The entire island equals the fraction $\frac{3}{3}$.

• _____ $\frac{2}{3}$ from _____.

Try Use a drawing or compute to show your work. Write your answer as a complete sentence.

Did you know?
The food that flamingos eat makes them turn pink in color.

_____

4. A flamingo egg is 2.3 inches wide and 3.7 inches long. Is the length more than twice the width? ◂MTK 27

Plan Fill in the blanks.

• The length is _____.

• The width is _____.

• _____ times the width equals 4.6.

• Compare the measures.

Try Use a drawing or compute to show your work. Write your answer as a complete sentence.

more ▸

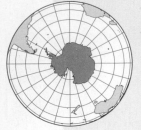

Sometimes problems have either too little or too much information.

You fly to the Antarctic to learn more about the penguins. To your surprise, you are told that only two species are native to the Antarctic. The rest actually live in warmer climates.

Although cartoons sometimes show penguins with Eskimos and polar bears, penguins are not native to the North Pole.

5. In the Antarctic, the Emperor Penguin stands about 1 meter tall and weighs up to 41 kilograms. The smallest penguin is the Little Blue, which weighs less than 1 kilogram. How does the Emperor Penguin compare in weight with the Little Blue? ◀MTK 347, 359

Plan Fill in the blanks.

- The Emperor Penguin weighs up to _____.

- The Little Blue weighs less than _____.

- _____ the two weights.

Try Use a drawing or compute to show your work.
Write your answer as a complete sentence.

_____

6. Most penguin eggs hatch between 42 and 48 days after being laid. Will the eggs laid on June 30 hatch by the end of July?

Plan Fill in the blanks.

- Most penguin eggs hatch between _____ and _____ days.

- Find the number of _____ in July.

Try Use a drawing or compute to show your work.
Write your answer as a complete sentence.

_____

Vocabulary ▾ meter (m) ▾ kilogram (kg)

Oman

7. You travel to Oman to see the wonderful birds there. You want to send each of your friends a letter. You need 30 stamps. There are 12 stamps on each sheet. How many sheets do you need to buy? ◂MTK 90, 175

Plan Fill in the blanks.

- You need a total of _____ stamps.

- There are _____ stamps on each sheet.

- Skip count by _____ to find the number of sheets you need.

Try Use a drawing or compute to show your work. Write your answer as a complete sentence.

_____

8. Look at the table. Were more new bird stamps produced in 1998 and 1999 or in 2001 and 2002? ◂MTK 268, 150–151

Year	New Bird Stamps Produced
2002	857
2001	1197
2000	1120
1999	1346
1998	996

Plan Fill in the blanks.

- Add 1197 and _____.

- Add 996 and _____.

- Compare the numbers to find the greater sum.

Try Use a drawing or compute to show your work. Write your answer as a complete sentence.

_____

65

There is often more than one good plan for solving a problem.

You decide to learn about birds of prey before writing your riddle.

Birds of prey have strong feet with talons and they eat meat. Most birds of prey catch their food while in flight.

Read each problem. Then follow the directions.

1. An eagle has 8 talons in all. They have 2 feet and the same number of talons on each foot. How many talons to they have on each foot? ◀MTK 76

Plan _____

_____

Try Draw or compute to show your work. Write your answer as a complete sentence.

_____

2. You see an eagle's nest that is 15 feet tall. Is the height of the nest more or less than four times the height of a student who is 4 feet tall? ◀MTK 62

The national bird of the United States is the bald eagle.

Plan _____

_____

Try Draw or compute to show your work. Write your answer as a complete sentence.

_____

66

Use the bar graph for problems 3–4.

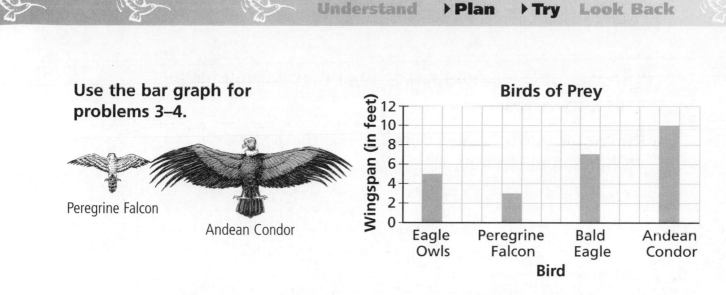

Peregrine Falcon

Andean Condor

Birds of Prey

3. Imagine that a Peregrine Falcon and an Andean Condor stood side-by-side with their wings wide open. How many times longer is the condor's wingspan than the falcon's wingspan? ◂MTK 76, 273

Plan _____

_____

Try Draw or compute to show your work. Write your answer as a complete sentence.

_____

4. Suppose the Museum of Natural History wants to exhibit life-size models of the 4 birds of prey in one display case. Each bird will stand wingtip to wingtip. At least how much space should be set aside in the display case? ◂MTK 36, 273

Plan _____

_____

Try Draw or compute to show your work. Write your answer as a complete sentence.

_____

more ▸

If your plan gives you an answer that doesn't make sense, try a new plan.

Don't give up. If one plan doesn't work, think of another way to find the answer.

Did you know?
Owls fly so quietly that other animals don't hear them coming. This is one reason they are such good hunters.

5. A Barn Owl can eat up to 3 mice each night. Over the course of a year, or 365 days, would that total about 1,000 mice? ◄ MTK 62

Plan _____

_____

Try Draw or compute to show your work. Write your answer as a complete sentence.

_____

6. The fossil of an Andean Condor from over 2 million years ago had a wingspan of 24 feet. How many 8-foot-long cars could you line up along its wingspan? ◄ MTK 76

Plan _____

_____

Try Draw or compute to show your work. Write your answer as a complete sentence.

_____

Use the bar graph.

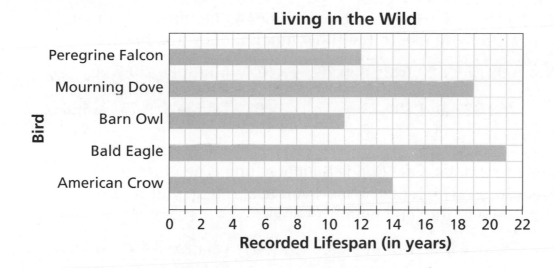

Living in the Wild

Bird / Recorded Lifespan (in years)

Peregrine Falcon, Mourning Dove, Barn Owl, Bald Eagle, American Crow

0 2 4 6 8 10 12 14 16 18 20 22

7. How many years difference is there between the lifespan of a Bald Eagle and a Barn Owl? ◂MTK 48, 273

Plan _____

_____

Try Draw or compute to show your work. Write your answer as a complete sentence.

_____

You have learned so much about birds. Now you get to name your favorite bird and tell why.

Favorite bird: _____

I like this bird because: ___ _____

_____

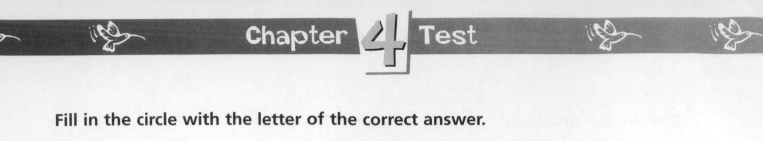

Fill in the circle with the letter of the correct answer.

1. Mia had $39.75. Her neighbor paid her $20 to mow the lawn. Which plan would you use to find how much money Mia has now?

    Ⓐ Subtract $20 from $39.75. Ⓒ Multiply $39.75 by $20.

    Ⓑ Add $20 and $39.75. Ⓓ Divide $39.75 by $20.

2. Luis has 2 dogs. One dog is 8 inches long. The other dog is 3 feet long. Which plan would you use to help you find the difference in the lengths of the dogs?

    Ⓐ Change 3 feet to inches. Add 8 inches to answer.

    Ⓒ Change 3 feet to inches. Subtract 8 inches from the answer.

    Ⓑ Change 3 feet to inches. Add 2 dogs to the answer.

    Ⓓ Change 3 feet to inches. Multiply 8 inches by the answer.

3. Shira takes 48 photos on her trip. She puts them in an album with 6 photos on each page. How many pages in the photo album does she use?

    Ⓐ 54 pages

    Ⓑ 42 pages

    Ⓒ 8 pages

    Ⓓ 288 pages

    Write or draw your plan here.

4. Kendra is mixing birdfeed. She needs $\frac{2}{3}$ cup of peanuts. She has $\frac{1}{3}$ cup. How much more does she need?

    Ⓐ $\frac{3}{3}$ cup

    Ⓑ $\frac{1}{3}$ cup

    Ⓒ $\frac{2}{9}$ cup

    Ⓓ $\frac{3}{6}$ cup

    Write or draw your plan here.

Choose the letter of the best answer. Then write why you made that choice.

5. On Monday, Mr. Martinez buys 7.3 gallons of gasoline. The next day he buys another 2.7 gallons. On both days he pays $1.39 a gallon. How much did he pay for gasoline on those 2 days? ◂MTK 179

(A) $2.78 _____

(B) $10.00 _____

(C) $12.00 _____

(D) $13.90 _____

6. At rest, a Hummingbird's heart beats about 500 times a minute. If startled, its heartbeat can rise to over 1,200 times a minute. How much faster is the startled heartbeat?

(A) more than twice _____

(B) more than three times _____

(C) more than 500 times _____

(D) more than 1,200 times _____

Write your plan and show your work.

7. Mansun's new flowerbed is 12 feet long and 8 feet wide. Last year, the flowerbed was only half this length and half this width. How much larger is the area of the new flowerbed? ◂MTK 350

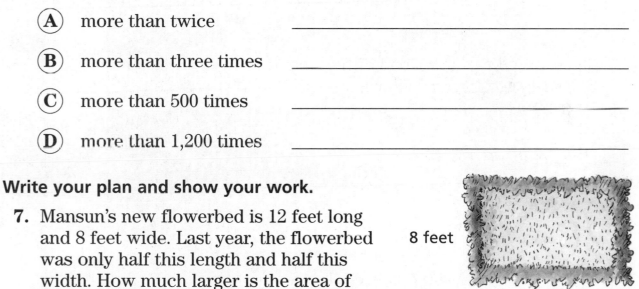

8 feet

12 feet

Write your plan here.   **Show your work here.**

_____

_____

_____

5

Treasures
from the Deep
Looking Back

Annual History Fair
this year's theme:

Shipwrecks and Treasures

Use your imagination
to create
a tabletop presentation
about 1 or more
historical shipwrecks.

Have fun and good luck!

In this chapter, you will collect information about shipwrecks and their treasures. You'll *look back* at shipwrecks from long ago. You'll also learn lots of different ways to *look back* at a math problem to check your work after you've solved it. You will practice using the fourth step of the four-step problem-solving method: **Look Back.**

There are four different ways divers explore shipwrecks on the ocean floor.

▲ An air tank allows a diver to breathe underwater.

▾ Small submarines can carry people to the remains of a sunken ship.

▲ Remote control robots can explore ships and places that are unsafe for people to go.

▸ Deep-sea divers wear special suits to protect them from the cold and to keep proper air pressure. Fresh air is supplied through tubes connected to the ship above.

73

Always look back to make sure you answered the question.

You want to participate in this year's History Fair. You go to the library to look up shipwrecks and treasures.

You read in a book that treasure diver Kip Wagner's nephew found a gold chain necklace with a dragon on it. The chain washed up on a beach in Florida. It is supposed to have over 1000 links on it. *Exactly how many links are on the chain,* you wonder.

On the Internet, you find a helpful website.

Sitting at the keyboard, you type:

> How many links are on the gold chain necklace that Kip Wagner's nephew found?
>
> **Ask**

The following answer appears:

WEB RESULTS

The necklace was found in 1962. It had been in the ocean for over 250 years before it beached in Florida.

The information tells you something about the necklace, but it doesn't answer your question.

Searching for information on the Internet can give you lots of data—some of it may be useful, while other data might be interesting but not helpful. As a result, you often have to go back to your original question and search again. In the end, you find that there are 2176 links on the necklace.

When you solve a word problem, it is important to always ▶ **Look Back** at the problem to be sure you answered the question asked.

Circle the choice that will best help you answer the question asked.

1. The necklace with the dragon on it sold for $50,000. In 1963, the *Real Eight* found a gold disk that sold for $17,500. A local antique shop wants to know what was the difference in the selling price of the gold disk and the necklace? ◀ MTK 17, 166–167, 171

Piece of Eight

   A. Find the year the necklace with the dragon was located.

   B. Find the difference between the selling price of the gold disk and the necklace.

   C. Find the year the gold disk was located.

   Did you know?
   Kip Wagner's company, *Real Eight*, searched for sunken treasures. *Real Eight* is named for the old Spanish coin called a *piece of eight*. The *Real Eight* explored the Spanish treasure fleet that sank in a hurricane off the coast of Florida in 1715.

2. Treasure diver Teddy Tucker found enough gold links to make a chain 20 feet long. Since 42 links weighed the same as one Portuguese coin called the *escudo*, he figured people used the links as money. How many links weighed the same as 3 escudos? ◀ MTK 174–175

   A. Find the number of links that weigh the same as 3 escudos.

   B. Find the age of the chain.

   C. Find the the age of each escudo.

3. A group of divers found a bag with 50 coins. There were 48 gold coins and 2 silver coins. Without looking, you reached into the bag and pulled out a coin. How likely is it that you would get a gold coin? ◀ MTK 292–293

   A. Find the age of each coin.

   B. Compare the number of gold coins to the number of silver coins.

   C. Find the weight of each coin.

   more ▶

Vocabulary ▾ likely

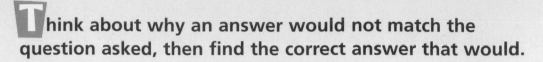

Think about why an answer would not match the question asked, then find the correct answer that would.

Treasure divers use grids to map the location of the treasures they find. In the grid, the ordered pair (4, 5) marks the spot where the bag of coins was found.

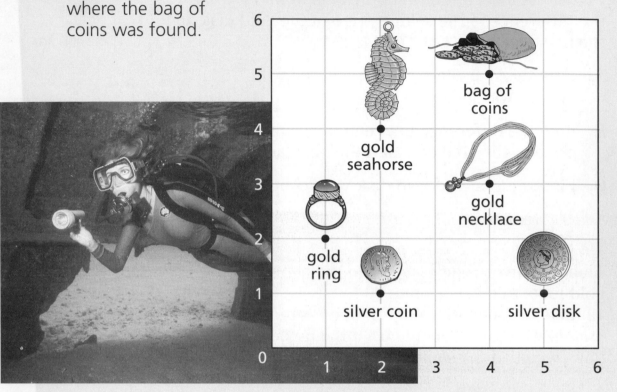

Circle the choice that will best help you answer the question asked.

4. What is the location of the gold ring? ◀MTK 258–259

   A. Find the ordered pair that names the location of the gold ring.

   B. Find the number of silver coins at location (2, 1).

   C. Find the number of items on the map.

5. Which treasure is in the location (4, 3)? ◀MTK 258–259

   A. Find the location of the ordered pair (3, 4).

   B. Find the location of the ordered pair (4, 3).

   C. Find the distance from (0, 0) to (4, 3).

Vocabulary ▼ grid ▼ ordered pair

This bar graph shows some of the treasures that the *Real Eight* found from one shipwreck.

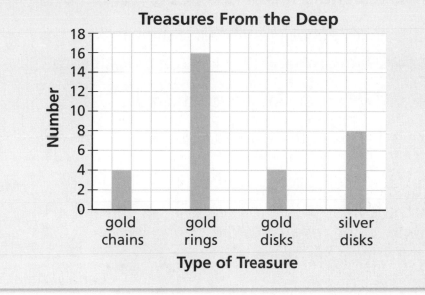

Treasures From the Deep

6. Which is greater—the number of gold disks or the number of silver disks found? ◂MTK 46–59, 273

   A. Look at the graph to see which bar is taller—the gold disks or the silver disks.

   B. Look at the graph to see how many items are listed in all.

   C. Look at the graph to see which bar is the tallest.

7. Use the information from the graph to write your own question. Then, write a sentence that would answer the question. ◂MTK 273

   _____

   _____

   _____

It's important to re-read a word problem after you're done, just to be sure you've answered the question.

Compare your answer with other numbers in a problem to eliminate answers that are not reasonable.

You want to learn about the following shipwrecks:

Mary Rose   *Titanic*   *Central America*

The three shipwrecks are located on the map.

The distance between the *Central America* and the *Mary Rose* is 4167 miles.

To find the distance between the *Titanic* and the *Mary Rose*, you use a ruler to draw a line from the *Mary Rose* to the *Titanic*. ◄MTK 305

Use the map and your line segment to help you answer each question.

1. Is the distance between the *Mary Rose* and the *Titanic more than* or *less than* the distance between the *Central America* and the *Mary Rose*? ◄MTK 435–436

   _____ **less than** _____

2. Is the distance between the *Mary Rose* and the *Titanic more than* or *less than* 4167 miles? ◄MTK 435–436, 446

   _____

3. Would 5240 miles be a reasonable estimate of the distance between the *Mary Rose* and the *Titanic*? ◄MTK 435–436, 446

   _____

4. Would 2330 miles be a reasonable estimate of the distance between the *Mary Rose* and the *Titanic*? ◄MTK 435–436, 446

   _____

Vocabulary ▼ distance

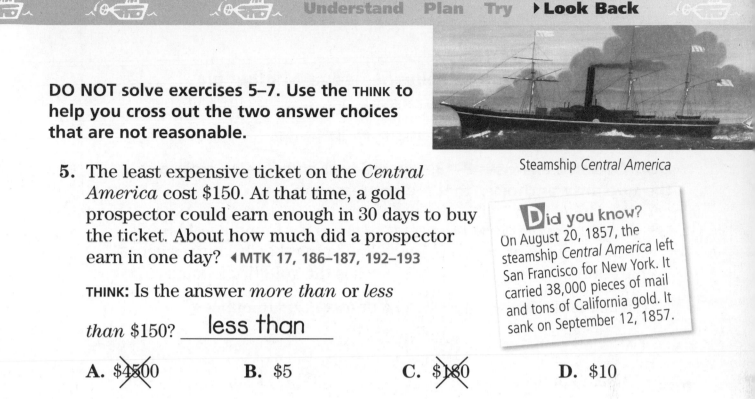

Steamship *Central America*

DO NOT solve exercises 5–7. Use the THINK to help you cross out the two answer choices that are not reasonable.

5. The least expensive ticket on the *Central America* cost $150. At that time, a gold prospector could earn enough in 30 days to buy the ticket. About how much did a prospector earn in one day? ◀MTK 17, 186–187, 192–193

THINK: Is the answer *more than* or *less than* $150? __less than__

Did you know?
On August 20, 1857, the steamship *Central America* left San Francisco for New York. It carried 38,000 pieces of mail and tons of California gold. It sank on September 12, 1857.

A. $~~4500~~   B. $5   C. $~~180~~   D. $10

6. In 1983, divers began to search for the *Central America*. A 1400-square mile search area was identified. The area of Rhode Island is 1545 square miles. By how many square miles is the area of Rhode Island greater? ◀MTK 160, 350–351

THINK: Is the answer *greater than* or *less than* 1545 square miles? _____

A. 2945 square miles   C. 1983 square miles

B. 145 square miles   D. 200 square miles

7. A robot named *Nemo* was used to explore the *Central America*. The *Nemo* was 15 feet long by 8 feet wide. What is the difference between its length and width? ◀MTK 46–59, 346

THINK: Is the answer *more than* or *less than* 15 feet?

_____

A. 19 feet   B. 5 feet   C. 7 feet   D. 23 feet

more ▶

DO NOT solve exercises 8–13. Use the THINK to help you cross out the two answer choices that are not reasonable.

8. Divers who explored the *Central America* found a gold brick that weighed about 46 pounds. You know that 16 ounces equal 1 pound. About how many ounces is the gold brick equal to? ◄ MTK 358

   THINK: Is the answer *more than* or *less than* 16 ounces?

   _____

   A. 2.88 ounces   **C.** 146 ounces

   B. 16 ounces   **D.** 736 ounces

9. Divers also found 3-ounce gold nuggets. On one dive, they collected 2 dozen similar nuggets. How many ounces did the 2 dozen nuggets weigh? ◄ MTK 180–181

   THINK: Is the answer *more than* or *less than* 3 ounces?

   _____

   A. 1 ounce   **C.** 24 ounces

   B. 2 ounces   **D.** 72 ounces

10. The explorers of the *Central America* identified 12 sea animals that have never been seen before. They also recognized 138 sea animals that are known. How many different kinds of sea animals did the *Central America* explorers come across? ◄ MTK 147–148

    THINK: Is the answer *more than* or *less than* 138 kinds

    of animals? _____

    A. 100 animals   **C.** 155 animals

    B. 150 animals   **D.** 126 animals

11. The *Erie* sank in 1841 with $10,000 cash on board. In 1854, divers retrieved $2,000. In 1960, divers found another $1,200. How much of the money was never found? ◂MTK 146–147, 158, 166–167, 171

THINK: Is the answer *more than* or *less than* $10,000?

_____

A. $6,800   **B.** $12,000   **C.** $6,000   **D.** $13,200

12. In the summer of 1940, the steamer *Niagara* sank in the Pacific Ocean. In the cargo hold was $12 million in gold bullion. So far, expert divers have retrieved about $9 million. About how much money still remains on the ocean floor? ◂MTK 17, 160

THINK: Is the answer *more than* or *less than* $12 million?

_____

A. $108 million   **B.** $21 million   **C.** $3 million   **D.** $9 million

13. A collection tray is 5 squares wide by 6 squares long. Divers put one coin in each square. How many squares are in the collection tray? ◂MTK 60–72, 350

Treasure divers use collection trays to keep track of where each treasure is found.

THINK: Is the answer *more than* or *less than* 6 squares? _____

A. 11 squares   **B.** 30 squares   **C.** 2 squares   **D.** 5 squares

14. In exercise 13, how did you decide whether your answer was *more than* or *less than* 6 squares?

_____

_____

_____

Always look back to be sure you've correctly labeled your answer.

The *Titanic* made its first and only trip in 1912. Although nicknamed *The Unsinkable Ship,* it sank on April 15. In 1986, Dr. Robert Ballard used a small submarine named *Alvin* to explore the sunken ocean liner.

You decide to go on the *Alvin* to visit the *Titanic* on the ocean floor. You hear someone talking but you could not hear clearly.

Now, was that $2\frac{1}{2}$ seconds or $2\frac{1}{2}$ hours, you wonder.

There is a big difference between $2\frac{1}{2}$ seconds and $2\frac{1}{2}$ hours. You want to know which is the correct time. Labels are also very important when you answer a math problem.

To reach the *Titanic,* it will take $2\frac{1}{2}$. . .

Choose the correct label from the box to answer exercises 1–3.

1. Ballard's group raised part of the *Titanic* 12,260 feet. This was still 200 feet below the surface. How deep was the *Titanic* before Ballard raised it? ◀MTK 146–147, 346

| feet |
| miles |
| deep |

Answer 12,460 _____

2. The *Real Eight* found 2 gold rings in one shipwreck and 16 gold rings in another shipwreck. How many gold rings did they find in all? ◀MTK 146–147

   > gold rings
   > shipwrecks
   > ounces

   Answer 18 _____

3. The *Real Eight* found a silver disk 18 inches in diameter. What was the radius of the disk? ◀MTK 85, 316, 346

   > silver disks
   > diameter
   > inches

   Answer 9 _____

Write the correct label to answer exercises 4–6.

4. The *Real Eight* found 2 large gold disks. Each disk weighed about $7\frac{1}{2}$ pounds. How much did the gold disks weigh in all? ◀MTK 230–231, 358

   Answer 15 _____

5. The oldest canoe found in Lake Phelps dates back more than 4000 years. The youngest canoe was 600 years old. What is the difference in the ages of the oldest and youngest canoes? ◀MTK 166–167

   Answer 3400 _____

   > **D**id you know?
   > In Lake Phelps, North Carolina, 26 Native American canoes were found. The canoes were made from logs and burned-out in the middle. The burned part was scraped clean to make space for passengers.

6. When the *Niagara* sank, the passengers and crew went into lifeboats. Someone in an airplane saw the lifeboats at 7:30 A.M., by 11:00 A.M. everyone was rescued. How long did it take from the time the lifeboats were sighted to the end of the rescue? ◀MTK 338–339

   Answer $3\frac{1}{2}$ _____

An estimate can help you decide whether your answer is about the right size.

Having a rough idea of what the correct answer should be is helpful when you need to decide between different answer choices.

Follow the steps to rule out answer choices that are not reasonable.

1. Divers searching for the gold bullion on the steamship *Niagara* used explosives to break down barriers. In one blast, they made an opening about $8\frac{1}{2}$ feet high by $4\frac{1}{2}$ feet wide. If this were a rectangle, what would be the perimeter of the opening? ◀MTK 143, 349

   Circle the choice that gives the best estimate of the perimeter.

   A. $10 + 5$ **B.** $10 + 5 + 10 + 5$ **C.** 8×4

   What is your estimate for the answer? About _____ feet

   Use your estimate to cross out two choices that are not reasonable.

   A. 2 feet **B.** 15 feet **C.** 26 feet **D.** 30 feet

---

2. The English warship *Mary Rose* sank in 1545. A crane was used to lift the ship out of the water 437 years later. In what year was the *Mary Rose* lifted out of the water? ◀MTK 130, 132–133, 344

   Circle the choice that gives the best estimate of when the *Mary Rose* was lifted out of the water.

   A. $1500 - 400$ **B.** $1600 + 500$ **C.** $1500 + 400$

   What is your estimate for the answer? Around the year _____

   Use your estimate to cross out two choices that are not reasonable.

   A. 1801 **B.** 1982 **C.** 1100 **D.** 1999

The table shows the lengths of some of the ships that have sunk.

On the Ocean Floor

Name of Ship	Ship Length
Central America	278 feet
Mary Rose	130 feet
Niagara	543 feet
Titanic	882 feet

Use the table for exercises 3–4.

3. How much longer is the *Titanic* than the *Central America*? ◀MTK 130, 132–133, 346

Circle the choice that gives the best estimate of the difference.

A. $900 - 300$ **B.** $900 + 300$ **C.** $900 \div 300$

What is your estimate for the answer? About _____ feet

Use your estimate to cross out two choices that are not reasonable.

A. 1160 feet   **B.** 614 feet   **C.** 398 feet   **D.** 604 feet

---

4. If all four ships in the table were lined up end to end, how long would the line of ships be? ◀MTK 130, 132–133, 346

Circle the choice that gives the best estimate of the length.

A. $300 + 100 + 500$ **B.** $300 + 100 + 500 + 900$ **C.** $300 + 900$

What is your estimate for the answer? About _____ feet

Use your estimate to cross out two choices that are not reasonable.

A. 1685 feet   **B.** 1800 feet   **C.** 1833 feet   **D.** 2000 feet

more ▶

An estimate can help you rule out unreasonable choices.

You have been working hard collecting as much information about historic shipwrecks as you need for the History Fair project. Now it is time to put all the data together.

Follow the steps to rule out answer choices that are not reasonable.

5. At the print shop, it costs $2.65 to print one page of your report on special paper. Your report is 13 pages long. How much will it cost in all? ◀MTK 136–137

Circle the choice that gives the best estimate of the cost.

A. $3 + 10   **B.** $3 × 10   **C.** 10 ÷ $3

What is your estimate for the answer? About _____

Use your estimate to cross out two choices that are not reasonable.

A. $15.65   **B.** $4.91   **C.** $34.45   **D.** $45.00

---

6. To create your presentation, you had to buy some supplies. How much is the total cost? ◀MTK 179

Circle the choice that gives the best estimate of the total cost.

A. $13 + $3 + $5 + $12

B. $13 × $3 × $5 × $12

C. $12 ÷ $3

What is your estimate for the answer?

About _____

Need to buy:	
Tri-fold board	$12.50
Spray glue	$3.45
Color construction paper	$4.75
Scissors	$11.80

Use your estimate to cross out two choices that are not reasonable.

A. $12   **B.** $30.50   **C.** $150   **D.** $32.50

Good news! Your presentation was a big hit. Everyone loved all the photographs and interesting information you included on your tri-fold board.

7. Time to celebrate! You spend $32.75 on invitations to invite 23 friends to a party. How much did each invitation cost? ◂MTK 139

Circle the choice that gives the best estimate of the cost.

A. $30 × 20   **B.** $30 ÷ 20   **C.** 20 ÷ $30

What is your estimate for the answer? About _____

Use your estimate to cross out two choices that are not reasonable.

A. $1.42   **B.** $753.25   **C.** $32.75   **D.** $2.00

8. A total of 16 friends will attend the party. You have 64 replicas of gold coins from a shipwreck. You want to divide the gold coins equally among your friends. How many coins will each guest get? ◂MTK 130, 139

Circle the choice that gives the best estimate of the answer.

A. 60 × 20   **B.** 60 ÷ 20   **C.** 60 + 20

What is your estimate for the answer? About _____ coins

Use your estimate to cross out two answer choices that are not reasonable.

A. 6 coins   **B.** 4 coins   **C.** 48 coins   **D.** 80 coins

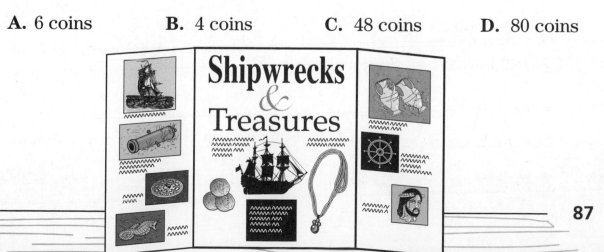

Fill in the circle with the letter of the correct answer.

1. Ella measures the diameter of the view port on the cruise liner. Which of the following might be the diameter?

   (A) 12 cubic inches   (C) 12 inches

   (B) 12 square inches   (D) 12 hours

2. The juice vendor has 32 oranges. She uses 16 to fill one order. Which of the following best describes the number of oranges left?

   (A) Fewer than 32   (C) More than 32

   (B) 32   (D) 0

3. Tessa worked on a long-term project 2 hours every day for 4 days. Which unit describes the amount of time she spent on the project?

   (A) projects   (C) inches

   (B) cups   (D) None of the above

4. Eric read 22 books in one year and 39 books the next year. How many books did he read in those 2 years?

   (A) 20 books   (C) 10 books

   (B) 40 books   (D) 61 books

Fill in the circle with the letter of the correct answer. Tell why you made your choice.

5. Carter walked $1\frac{1}{4}$ miles on the treadmill on Monday. Then he walked another $2\frac{3}{4}$ miles on Tuesday. How many miles did he walk in all?

   (A) 3 miles _____

   (B) 1 mile _____

   (C) 4 miles _____

   (D) 2 miles _____

For problems 6–8, write the answer on the lines provided.

6. There are 6 cars and 30 people. An equal number of people go in each car. Write a multiplication or division expression that tells how many people are in each car.

   _____

Write your plan and show your work

7. Angel Waterfall in Venezuela is about 3300 feet high. You know that 3 feet equal 1 yard. About how many yards high is the waterfall?

   _____   **Show your work here.**

   _____

   _____

8. Write two ways that you can look back to check the answer to a problem.

   1) _____

   2) _____

Chapter 6

A Towering Contest
Putting It All Together

Build a Tower Contest

Simon Rodia came from Italy to the United States. He was a builder and in his free time built the Watts Towers in Los Angeles. It is listed on the National Register of Historic Places.

In 1985 a contest was held in Los Angeles to build a model that reflected the spirit of the Watts Towers. Three prizes of $1000, $500, and $250 were awarded. The designs were very imaginative. One of the award-winning designs even had a floating half-orange in it.

Our newspaper is holding a contest in honor of the Watts Towers. We are looking for designs inspired by the towers. There are many problems to be solved when building and designing a tower. So, sharpen your problem solving skills, be creative, and enter the contest today.

In this chapter, you will see that building a tower is not simple. An organized method is needed. You'll learn how an organized method can also help you solve math problems. You'll put together all the skills you've learned so far to see how the four-step problem-solving method (**Understand, Plan, Try,** and **Look Back**) can help you become a better problem solver.

◀ Simon Rodia was a craftsman. He used objects such as soda bottles, tiny pebbles, seashells, and colored rocks to build his gigantic work of art.

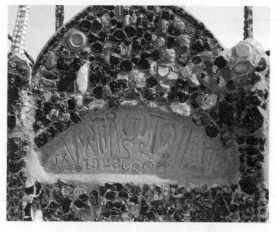

▼ Simon Rodia put SR in many places on the towers. It was his way of signing his work.

▼ Many people say that the Watts Towers have a jazzy, upbeat feel. Today, it is home to the Watts Towers Jazz Festival.

▲ The Watts Towers have inspired similar towers all over the world, for example, the Spittelau Heating Plant in Austria.

Now it's time to apply what you've learned.

You decide to visit the Watts Towers in Los Angeles to get inspiration for your own tower design.

You learn that Simon Rodia had a vision to do something big for his community. That took a lot of organizing and planning. He spent 33 years building the Watts Towers.

He planned the towers in his head.

He collected things like seashells, pottery, colored glass, tile, corncobs, and rocks to put on the towers.

He ordered materials like cement and stone.

He put the towers on a solid foundation so they would last a long time.

He planned to make the towers so he could climb on them without using a ladder. He built a ring and then stood on it to make the ring above. The distance between each ring is about the height Simon could reach with his out-stretched arms. This made it easy to climb from one level to the next.

As you can see, building a tower requires a lot of planning and an organized method. When you solve math problems, you also need an organized method. You can use this four-step problem-solving method.

FOUR-STEP PROBLEM-SOLVING METHOD

Step 1 ▸ **Understand** the problem.

Step 2 ▸ **Plan** how to solve the problem.

Step 3 ▸ **Try** your plan.

Step 4 ▸ **Look Back** at your solution to check it.

You've already learned about each of these four steps in this book.

Name the step or steps you learned in each chapter. Write a short summary of the problem-solving strategies.

Chapter 1 _____

_____

Chapter 2 _____

_____

Chapter 3 _____

_____

Chapter 4 _____

_____

Chapter 5 _____

_____

Now it's time to put all four steps together.

Sometimes a picture can help you decide which operation to use.

Problem In 1921, Simon Rodia began building the Watts Towers on a triangular piece of land. One side of the triangle is 151 feet long. Another side is 69 feet long. The last side is 137 feet long. What is the perimeter of this piece of land?

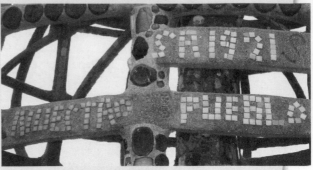

Simon Rodia put the name *Nuestro Pueblo* on the towers. *Nuestro Pueblo* means *Our Town* or *Our People* in Spanish.

Answer the questions to see how the four-step problem-solving method can be used to solve the problem.

▸ Understand

1. What does the problem ask you to find?

_____

2. Place a ✔ in the ☐ if that information is needed to solve the problem.

☐ The land is in the shape of a triangle.

☐ Simon Rodia started the Watts Towers in 1921.

☐ The lengths of the three sides of the triangle.

▸ Plan

3. Circle the choice that can help you find the perimeter of the land.

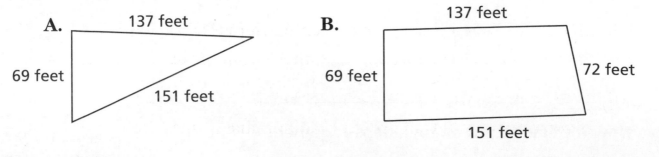

A.
137 feet
69 feet
151 feet

B.
137 feet
69 feet
72 feet
151 feet

94 Vocabulary ▼ triangle

4. Circle the plan you can use to solve the problem. ◀MTK 349

   Plan A

   • Multiply 151, 69, and 137.
   • The answer will be in cubic feet.

   Plan B

   • Add 151, 69, and 137.
   • The answer will be in feet.

   Plan C

   • Add 151, 69, and 137.
   • The answer will be in square feet.

▶**Try**

5. Show how you would carry out the plan. ◀MTK 150–151, 153

6. Write a sentence that answers the problem.

   _____

▶**Look Back**

7. Did you answer the question that was asked? _____
   If you answered *no*, go back and redo your work.

8. Circle a good estimate for the answer. ◀MTK 132–133

   A. $100 + 60 + 100 = 260$

   B. $150 + 70 + 140 = 360$

   C. $100 + 70 + 100 = 270$

9. Does your estimate show that your answer is reasonable? _____
   If you answered *no*, go back and check your work.

10. Does your answer have the correct label? _____
    If you answered *no*, go back and add or change the label.

more ▶

Sometimes you can use a simpler problem to help plan your solution.

Problem Simon Rodia bought bags of cement that weighed 94 pounds each. In the 1920s, each bag cost 20¢. How much did it cost him to buy 80 bags of cement?

Answer the questions to see how the four-step problem-solving method can be used to solve the problem.

▸**Understand**

11. What does the problem ask you to find?

_____

12. Place a ✔ in the ☐ if that information is needed to solve the problem.

☐ A bag of cement weighed 94 pounds.

☐ Each bag cost 20¢.

☐ Simon Rodia bought 80 bags.

▸**Plan**

13. Use this simpler problem to help you plan what to do.

Think!

Simpler problem A bag of cement costs **2¢**. How much does **8** bags of cement cost?

Draw a picture that describes the simpler problem.

Circle the expression that describes the simpler problem. ◂MTK 252
A. $8 \div 2$ **B.** 8×2 **C.** $8 + 2$ **D.** $8 - 2$

Circle the expression that describes the original problem. ◂MTK 252
A. $80 \div 20$ **B.** 80×20 **C.** $80 + 20$ **D.** $80 - 20$

▸**Try**

14. Circle the computation that correctly carries out the plan. ◂MTK 180–181

A.
$$20\overline{)80}\;{}^{4}$$
$$-\,80$$
$$\overline{0}$$

B.
$$80$$
$$\times\,20$$
$$\overline{1600}$$

C.
$$80$$
$$+\,20$$
$$\overline{100}$$

D.
$$80$$
$$-\,20$$
$$\overline{60}$$

15. Is your answer in cents (¢) or in dollars ($)? _____

16. Write a sentence that answers the problem.

_____

▸**Look Back**

17. Did you answer the question that was asked? _____
If you answered *no*, go back and redo your work.

18. Do you think your answer should be *more than* or *less than* 20¢?

_____

Is it? _____ If you answered *no*,
go back and check your work.

19. Does your answer have the correct label?

_____

If you answered *no*, go back and add or
change the label.

Simon Rodia spent over $3000 for
cement for the Center Tower.

more ▸

Sometimes the information you need is in a table or graph.

Problem What is the difference between the height of the East Tower and the height of the West Tower?

Height of the Watts Towers

Tower	Height
Center Tower	$99\frac{1}{2}$ feet
East Tower	55 feet
Gazebo Spire	40 feet
West Tower	$97\frac{3}{4}$ feet

Answer the questions to see how the four-step problem-solving method can be used to solve the problem.

▸ **Understand**

20. What does the problem ask you to find?

_____

21. Which numbers in the table will you use? Circle them. ◂ MTK 268

22. Is there any other information you need to solve the problem?

_____

If you answered *yes*, how can you find that information?

_____

▸ **Plan**

23. Complete the plan. Fill in each blank with a word from the box. ◂ MTK 234–235

Plan

Find the _____ between 55 feet and $97\frac{3}{4}$ feet.

The answer will be in _____.

add
subtract
multiply
divide
feet
inches
difference
to

▸**Try**

24. Show how to carry out the plan. ◂MTK 234–235

25. Write a sentence that answers the problem.

_____

_____

▸**Look Back**

26. Did you answer the question that was asked? _____
If you answered *no*, go back and redo your work.

27. Show how to estimate the answer. ◂MTK 132–133

28. Does your estimate show that your answer is reasonable?

_____

If you answered *no*, go back and check your work.

29. Does your answer have the correct label? _____
If you answered *no*, go back and add or change the label.

more ▸

Sometimes a problem has more information than you need.

Problem In 1959, the city of Los Angeles wanted to make sure the towers were safe. They said that the West Tower would have to hold a 10,000-pound load. Over 1000 people watched as engineers put a load of 10,000 pounds on the tower. The tower held and after that the Watts Towers were declared safe. A 10,000-pound load would be the same as how many 100-pound people?

Answer the questions to see how the four-step problem-solving method can be used to solve the problem.

▶ Understand

30. What does the problem ask you to find?

_____

_____

31. What information do you need to solve it?

_____

_____

_____

32. Is there any information that you don't need to solve the problem? If so, tell what information that is.

_____

▶ Plan

33. Write a plan for solving the problem. ◀ MTK 186–187

Plan

_____

_____

100

▸ Try

34. Show how you would carry out the plan. ◂MTK 186–187

35. Write a sentence that answers the problem.

_____

_____

▸ Look Back

36. Did you answer the question that was asked? _____
If you answered *no*, go back and redo your work.

37. Do you think your answer should be *more than* or *less than*

10,000 people? _____ Is it? _____
If you answered *no*, go back and check your work.

38. Explain how you decided whether your answer should be
more than or *less than* 10,000 people.

_____

_____

39. Does your answer have the correct label?

_____

If you answered *no*, go back and
add or change the label.

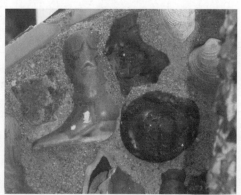

There are many unusual objects like a teapot spout
and a cowboy boot in the concrete of the Towers.

101

When solving problems on your own, you can always use the four-step method.

It won't solve the problem for you, but it can help you keep organized. Here are some questions to think about as you use this method.

▸ Understand

- Do I know what each word in the problem means? (If you don't know what a word means, use your handbook *Math to Know*, your math book, or a dictionary to help you.)
- What information do I have? What information do I need to solve the problem?
- Should my answer be an estimate or an exact number?
- Is there any information that is missing? If there is, can I find that information?
- Is there any information that I don't need?

▸ Plan

- Can I draw a picture to help me solve the problem?
- Can I write an expression that shows what the problem says?
- Can I solve a simpler similar problem that will help me solve the original problem?
- Do I need more than one step to solve the problem?

▸ Try

- Am I carrying out each step of my plan?
- Am I using the correct numbers from the problem?

▸ Look Back

- Did I answer the question that was asked?
- Did I label my answer correctly?
- Can I check whether my answer makes sense by comparing it to one of the other numbers in the problem?
- Can I use estimation to check whether my answer is reasonable?

Solve the problem. Explain how you used each of the four problem-solving steps. Use the questions on page 102 to help you.

1. Tours are given at the Watts Towers every half hour. On Saturdays the first tour starts at 10:30 A.M. and the last tour starts at 2:30 P.M. Each tour can have no more than 20 people on it. What is the greatest number of people that can tour the Watts Towers on a single Saturday? ◀MTK 174-175, 338

▶ **Understand**

_____

_____

▶ **Plan**

_____

_____

_____

▶ **Try**

Answer in a complete sentence.

_____

_____

▶ **Look Back**

_____

_____

_____

_____

more ▶

Use everything you have learned so far to solve the problems.

Solve the problem. Explain how you used each of the four problem-solving steps. Use the questions on page 102 to help you.

2. You have been staying with friends in Los Angeles for your visit to the Watts Towers. The drive to the towers is 57.3 miles. On your last day, you take another route to the towers that is 52.9 miles. What is the difference between the two distances? ◄MTK 168–169, 346

▸ **Understand**

_____

_____

▸ **Plan**

_____

_____

▸ **Try**

Did you know?
When Simon Rodia decided to leave Los Angeles, he gave the land and the towers to a neighbor.

Answer in a complete sentence.

_____

▸ **Look Back**

_____

_____

_____

3. You have designed your tower. You go to a lumberyard to buy some wood to begin making it. You buy one board that is $4\frac{1}{2}$ feet long and another board that is $1\frac{1}{2}$ feet long. How many $\frac{1}{2}$-foot pieces can you cut from these two boards? ◀ MTK 228, 232, 234, 346

▶ **Understand**

_____

_____

▶ **Plan**

_____

_____

▶ **Try**

Answer in a **complete sentence.**

_____

▶ **Look Back**

_____

_____

_____

Now you know how to use the four-step problem-solving method. You can use it whenever you solve math problems. You may want to keep this book handy, so that you can use the questions on pages 102 to help you.

Good luck and have fun solving problems!

Questions 1–5 are about this word problem:

Blong went to the store. He saw a sign saying the red pencils cost 10¢ apiece, the blue pencils cost 15¢ apiece, and the yellow pencils cost 12¢ apiece. He bought 1 yellow pencil and 3 blue pencils. How much money did he spend in all?

For questions 1–2, fill in the circle with the letter of the correct answer.

1. Which information is *not* needed to solve the problem?

  (**A**) Red pencils cost 10¢ apiece.

  (**B**) Blue pencils cost 15¢ apiece.

  (**C**) Yellow pencils cost 12¢ apiece.

2. Which plan would you use to solve the word problem?

  (**A**) **Plan A**

    • Add the cost of 1 blue pencil to the cost of 1 yellow pencil.

    • Add the cost of the 2 pencils to the cost of 1 red pencil.

  (**B**) **Plan B**

    • Multiply the cost of 1 blue pencil by 3 to find the cost of 3 blue pencils.

    • Add the cost of 3 blue pencils to the cost of 1 yellow pencil.

  (**C**) **Plan C**

    • Multiply the cost of 1 blue pencil by 3 to find the cost of 3 blue pencils.

    • Add the cost of 3 blue pencils, the cost of 1 yellow pencil, and the cost of 1 red pencil.

For questions 3–6, write your answer in the space provided.

3. Carry out the plan from question 2.

4. Write a sentence that gives the correct answer to the word problem.

_____

5. Explain how estimation can help you check the reasonableness of your answer in question 4.

_____

_____

_____

6. What are the problem-solving steps you learned in this book?

_____

_____

Name 3 reasons why you think the steps are helpful.

_____

_____

_____

_____

_____

Vocabulary

A A.M.

area (*A*)

about

average

angle

B bar graph

C cent (¢)

cost

change

cubic feet (ft³)

column

cup (c)

D data

diagram

degree (°)

diameter (*d*)

denominator

difference

distance

estimate

E equals (=)

exact

equation

expression

Fahrenheit (F)

fourth

first (*adj*)

fraction

foot *or* feet (ft)

gallon (gal)

graph

grid

greater than (>)

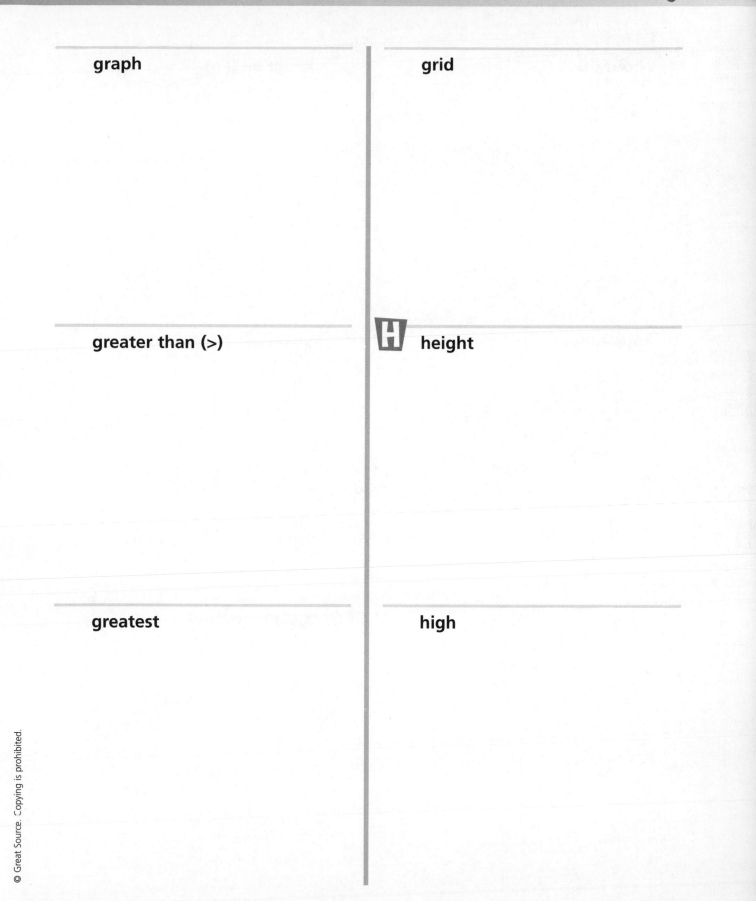 height

greatest

hour (h)

kilogram (kg)

hundred

kilometer (km)

inch (in.)

least

left

likely

length

line graph

less than (<)

line plot

long

meter (m)

M maximum

mile (mi)

measurement

miles per hour (mph)

million

minimum

minute (min)

N numerator

odd

one third

ordered pair

perimeter (*P*)

ounce (oz)

pictograph

P P.M.

pound (lb)

prism

quarter

product

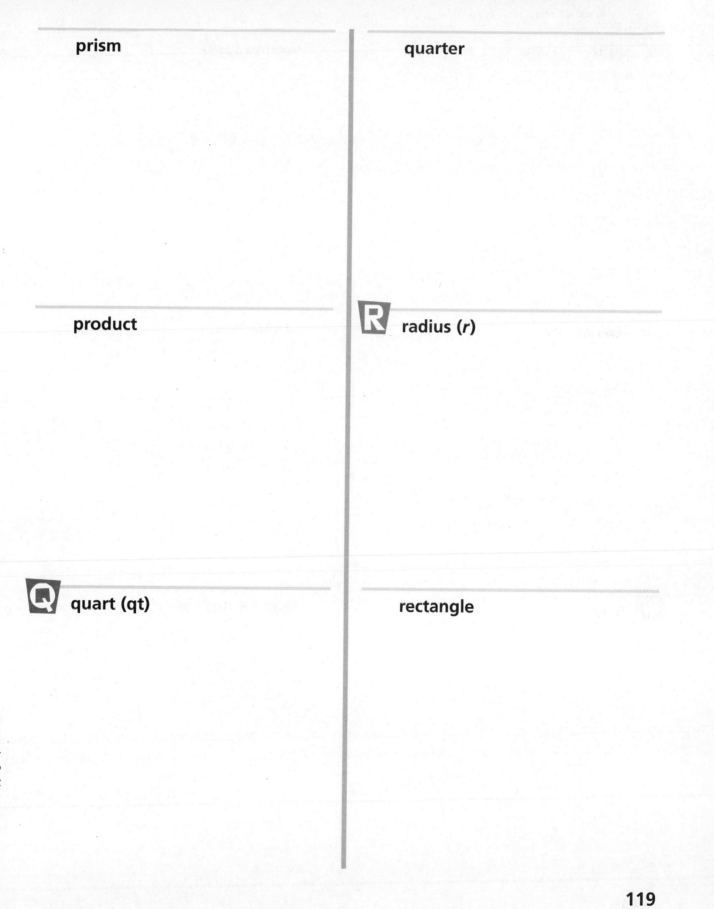 radius (r)

quart (qt)

rectangle

right

second (*adj*)

row

second (sec)

same

side

simplify

sum

square foot *or* feet (ft²)

T table

square mile (mi²)

temperature

thousand

triangle

ton (t)

twice

total

two thirds

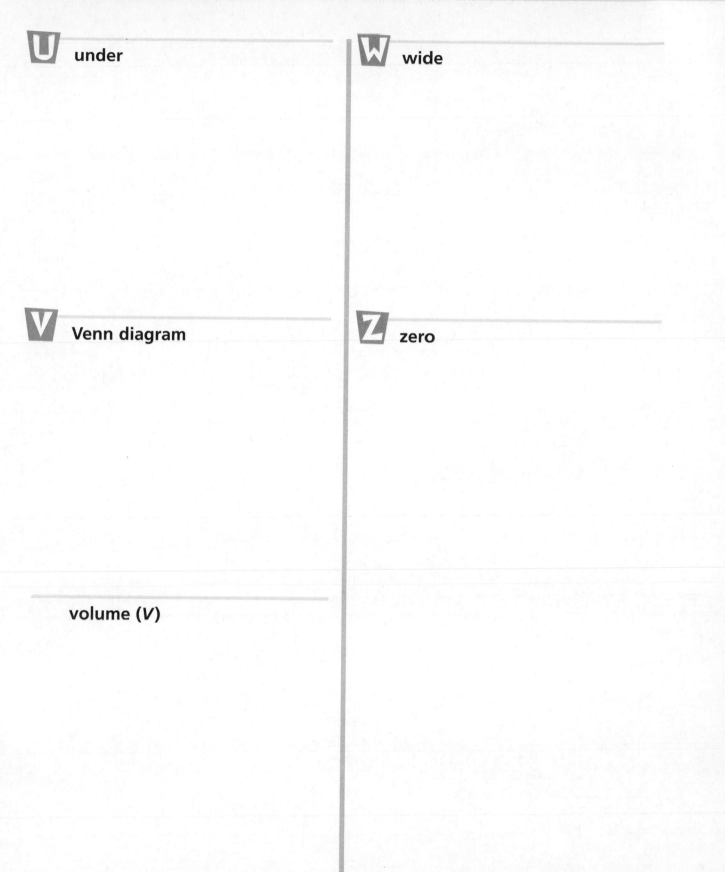

U under

W wide

V Venn diagram

Z zero

volume (*V*)